ATLAS OF CLASSICAL HISTORY

ATLAS OF
CLASSICAL HISTORY

Fifth edition

Michael Grant

New York

OXFORD UNIVERSITY PRESS

1994

© 1971, 1974, 1986, 1989, 1994 Michael Grant Publications Ltd

First published in Great Britain by
The Orion Publishing Group Limited
5 Upper St. Martin's Lane, London WC2H 9EA

Published in the United States of America by
Oxford University Press, Inc.
200 Madison Avenue
New York, N.Y. 10016, U.S.A.

Oxford is a registered trademark of
Oxford University Press

Library of Congress Cataloging-in-Publication Data
Grant, Michael, 1914–
    Atlas of classical history / Michael Grant.—[New rev. ed.]
      p. cm.
    Covers the Near East, ancient Egypt, Greece, and Rome; shows
    the period between 1700 BC and 565 AD.
    "First published in Great Britain by the Orion Publishing Group
    Limited ... London"—CIP t.p. verso.
    Rev. ed. of: Ancient history atlas/Michael Grant. 1974.
    Includes index.
    ISBN 0–19–521074–3 (hardback)
    ISBN 0–19–521078–6 (paperback)
    1. Geography, Ancient—Maps.   I. Grant, Michael, 1914–
Ancient history atlas. II. Title.
G1033.G65 1994 <G&M>
911'.3—dc20   93–48331
                                           CIP
                                         MAP

Printing (last digit): 9 8 7 6 5 4 3 2 1

Printed in Great Britain

Preface

This is an atlas of the classical world – the ancient Greek and Roman world, which needs to be understood if we are to understand the world of today. To say that such an atlas could ever be a substitute for a historical survey would be an exaggeration. Nevertheless, geography is such a vital, indeed predominant, factor in ancient history – and such a difficult factor because of all the changes of names[1] – that the whole course of events often seems to mean practically nothing without maps, and without a lot of them, carefully devised.

Older classical atlases, apart from a varying degree of emphasis on physical aspects, tended to concentrate on political themes, and it is true enough that these stand in great need of maps. But the present volume attempts to cast the net wider, and to introduce economic, cultural, religious and other topics as well. There are also a number of town plans.

Modern research in archaeology and other fields has shown that the classical world cannot be grasped without some appreciation of what went before it. I have consequently started this book with a number of maps illustrating the Mediterranean world during the second millennium BC, and particularly during the period from 1700 BC onwards, when the international scene had already assumed a well-defined and complex appearance; and the story is carried onwards to offer brief illustrations of the Old Testament. At the other end of the story, the traditional terminal date of the ancient world, the year AD 476 when the last western emperor ceased to reign, is again not a very meaningful landmark, so I have carried on the tale until the reign of Justinian in the following century.

It will clear enough what a very great deal is owed to the talent of Arthur Banks for transcribing the written and spoken world into cartographic form. I am also most grateful to Julian Shuckburgh and Benjamin Buchan for all the assistance they rendered on behalf of the publishers, and I want to thank Jane Dorner for assistance with the index and C. R. B. Elliott for help with an earlier revised edition. Finally, I have to acknowledge a substantial debt to existing classical atlases, German and English. And I must single out, for a special word of gratitude, the *Atlas of the Classical World* edited by A. A. M. van der Heyden and H. H. Scullard for Messrs Nelson, and *Westermanns Grosser Atlas zur Weltgeschichte* (Westermann, Braunschweig). N. G. L. Hammond's *Atlas of the Greek and Roman World in Antiquity* (Noyes Press, Park Ridge) is now fundamental; so is Routledge's new classical atlas.

For this fifth edition I have added new maps on the changing frontier of the Roman Empire (maps 72 and 73), on the persecution of the Christians (map 86) and on the Roman Empire in its final years (maps 88 and 90).

1994   MICHAEL GRANT

[1] Modern names are given after the ancient in the Index.

List of Maps

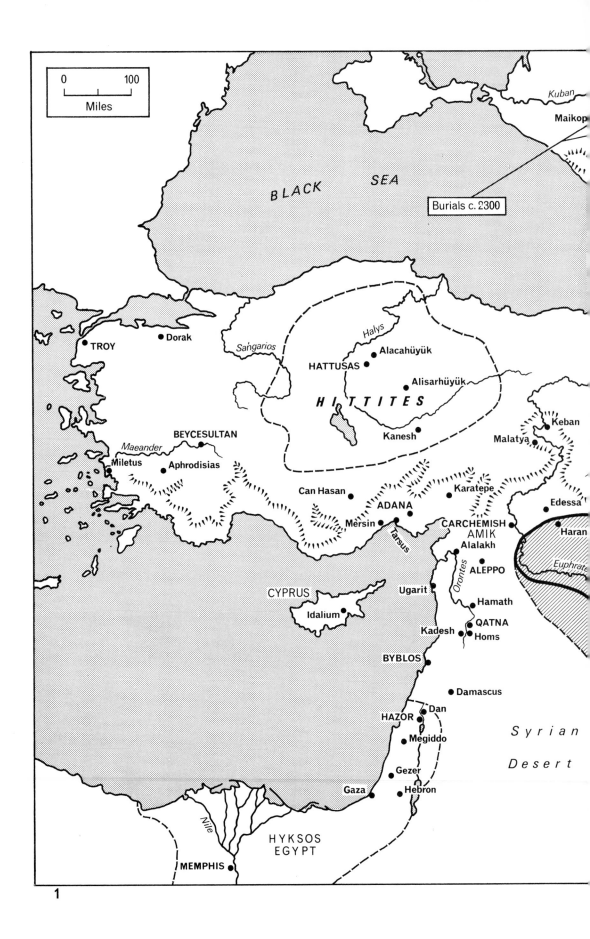

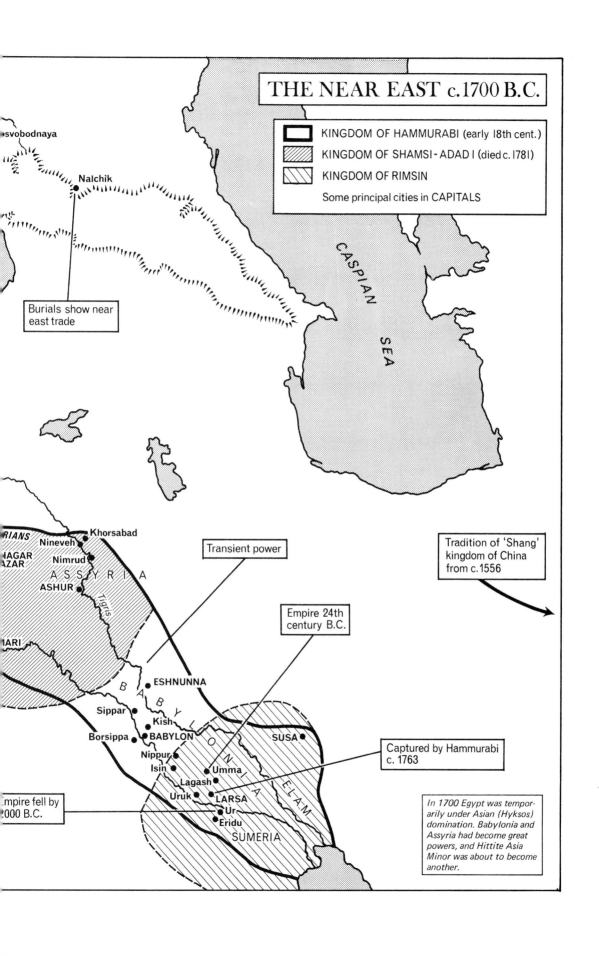

THE NEAR EAST c.1700 B.C.

☐ KINGDOM OF HAMMURABI (early 18th cent.)

▨ KINGDOM OF SHAMSI-ADAD I (died c.1781)

▨ KINGDOM OF RIMSIN

Some principal cities in CAPITALS

svobodnaya

Nalchik

Burials show near
east trade

CASPIAN SEA

RIANS

Khorsabad
Nineveh
HAGAR
AZAR
Nimrud
ASSYRIA
ASHUR

MARI

Tigris

Transient power

Tradition of 'Shang'
kingdom of China
from c.1556

Empire 24th
century B.C.

BABYLONIA

ESHNUNNA

Sippar

Kish

Borsippa   BABYLON   SUSA

Nippur
Isin   Umma
Lagash
Uruk   LARSA
Ur
Eridu
SUMERIA

ELAM

Captured by Hammurabi
c. 1763

Empire fell by
2000 B.C.

In 1700 Egypt was tempor-
arily under Asian (Hyksos)
domination. Babylonia and
Assyria had become great
powers, and Hittite Asia
Minor was about to become
another.

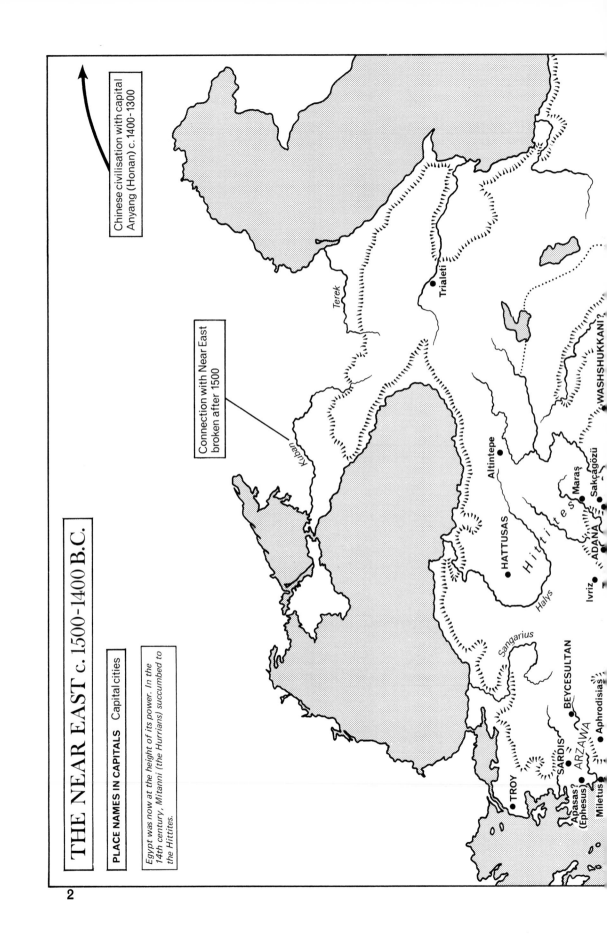

THE NEAR EAST c. 1500-1400 B.C.

PLACE NAMES IN CAPITALS   Capital cities

Egypt was now at the height of its power. In the 14th century, Mitanni (the Hurrians) succumbed to the Hittites.

Chinese civilisation with capital Anyang (Honan) c. 1400-1300

Connection with Near East broken after 1500

Terek

Kuban

Trialeti

Altıntepe

HATTUSAS

Hittites

Maraş

Sakçagözü

WASHSHUKKANI ?

Ivriz

ADANA

Halys

Sangarius

BEYCESULTAN

Aphrodisias ?

TROY

SARDIS

ARZAWA

Apasas ? (Ephesus)

Miletus

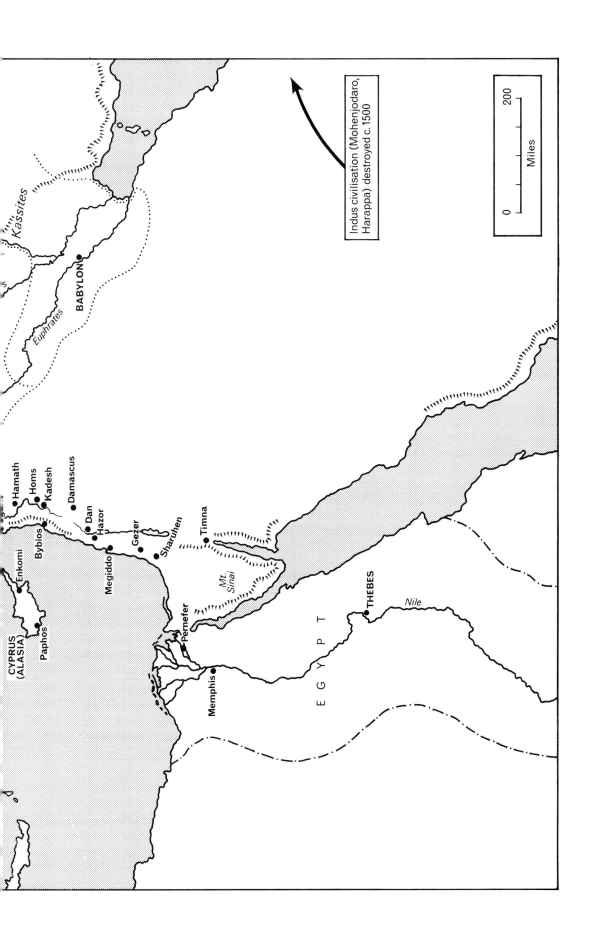

CYPRUS (ALASIA)

Paphos

Enkomi

Byblos

Hamath

Homs

Kadesh

Damascus

Dan

Hazor

Gezer

Sharuhen

Megiddo

Timna

Mt. Sinai

Pernefer

Memphis

E G Y P T

THEBES

Nile

BABYLON

Kassites

Euphrates

Indus civilisation (Mohenjodaro, Harappa) destroyed c.1500

0   200   Miles

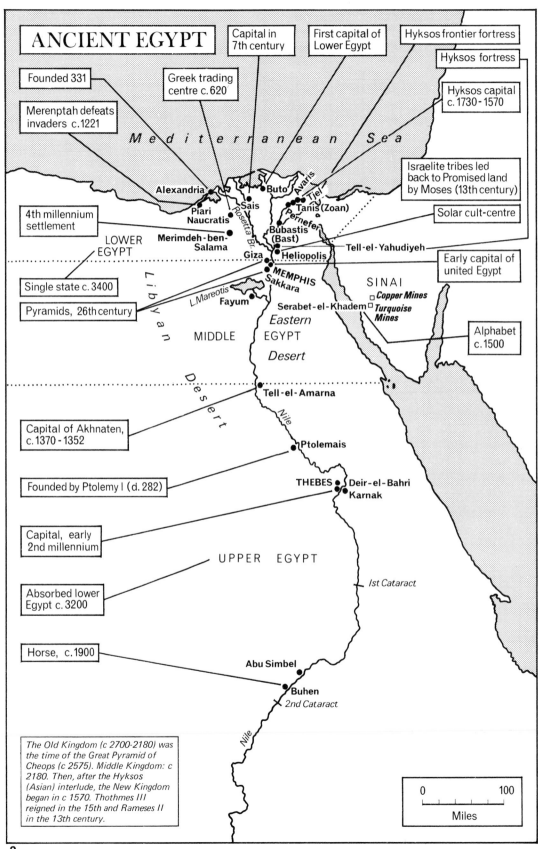

ANCIENT EGYPT

Capital in 7th century

First capital of Lower Egypt

Hyksos frontier fortress

Hyksos fortress

Greek trading centre c. 620

Hyksos capital c. 1730 - 1570

Founded 331

Merenptah defeats invaders c.1221

M e d i t e r r a n e a n   S e a

Israelite tribes led back to Promised land by Moses (13th century)

Solar cult-centre

Alexandria

Buto   **Avaris**

Tjel

4th millennium settlement

Piari
Naucratis

Sais

Tanis (Zoan)

Pernefer

LOWER EGYPT

Merimdeh-ben-Salama

Bubastis (Bast)

Tell-el-Yahudiyeh

Early capital of united Egypt

Giza   **Heliopolis**

Single state c. 3400

L.Mareotis

MEMPHIS
Sakkara

SINAI

□ **Copper Mines**

Pyramids, 26th century

Libyan

Fayum

Serabet-el-Khadem □ *Turquoise Mines*

Eastern

EGYPT

Alphabet c.1500

Desert

MIDDLE

Desert

Tell-el-Amarna

Capital of Akhnaten, c.1370 - 1352

Nile

Ptolemais

Founded by Ptolemy I (d. 282)

THEBES **Deir-el-Bahri**

Karnak

Capital, early 2nd millennium

UPPER EGYPT

Ist Cataract

Absorbed lower Egypt c. 3200

Horse, c.1900

Abu Simbel

Buhen
2nd Cataract

Nile

The Old Kingdom (c 2700-2180) was the time of the Great Pyramid of Cheops (c 2575). Middle Kingdom: c 2180. Then, after the Hyksos (Asian) interlude, the New Kingdom began in c 1570. Thothmes III reigned in the 15th and Rameses II in the 13th century.

0   100

Miles

3

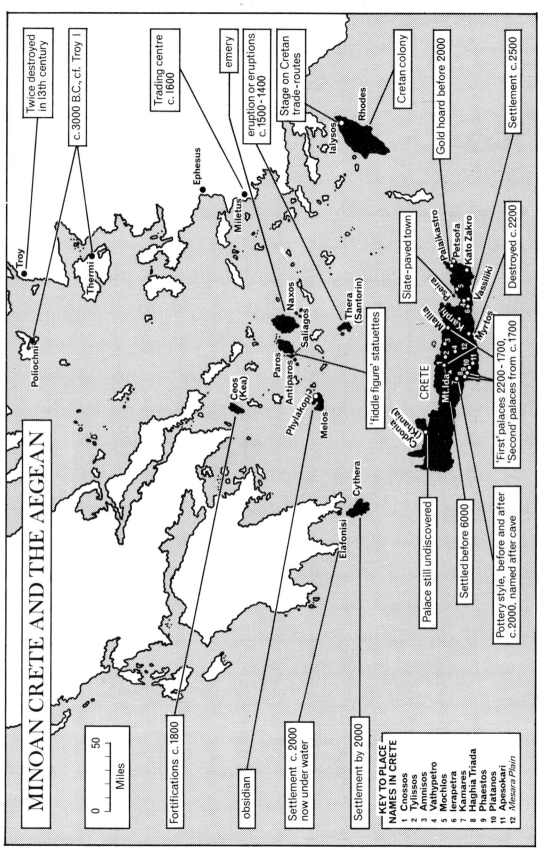

MINOAN CRETE AND THE AEGEAN

Twice destroyed in 13th century

c. 3000 B.C., cf. Troy I

Trading centre c. 1600

emery

eruption or eruptions c. 1500 - 1400

Stage on Cretan trade-routes

Cretan colony

Gold hoard before 2000

Settlement c. 2500

Destroyed c. 2200

Troy

Poliochni

Thermi

Ephesus

Miletus

Rhodes

Ialysos

Naxos

Paros
Antiparos
Saliagos

Thera (Santorin)

Ceos (Kea)

Phylakopi?

Melos

'fiddle figure' statuettes

Slate-paved town

Palaikastro
Petsofa
Kato Zakro

Vassiliki

Malia
Karphi
Pseira

Myrtos

CRETE

Mt. Ida

Cydonia (Khania)

Cythera

Elafonisi

Fortifications c. 1800

obsidian

Settlement c. 2000 now under water

Settlement by 2000

Palace still undiscovered

Settled before 6000

Pottery style, before and after c. 2000, named after cave

'First' palaces 2200 - 1700, 'Second' palaces from c. 1700

0   50
Miles

KEY TO PLACE NAMES IN CRETE
1 Cnossos
2 Tylissos
3 Amnisos
4 Vathypetro
5 Mochlos
6 Ierapetra
7 Kamares
8 Haghia Triada
9 Phaestos
10 Platanos
11 Apesokari
12 *Mesara Plain*

4

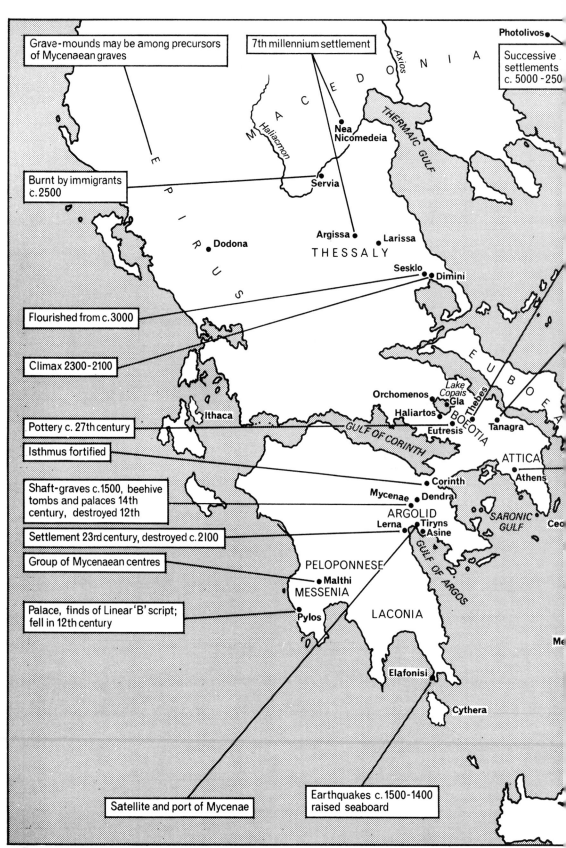

Grave-mounds may be among precursors of Mycenaean graves

7th millennium settlement

Successive settlements c. 5000 - 250

Photolivos

Axios

M A C E D O N I A

E

THERMAIC GULF

Haliacmon

Nea Nicomedeia

Burnt by immigrants c.2500

Servia

E P I R U S

Dodona

Argissa

Larissa

THESSALY

Sesklo

Dimini

Flourished from c.3000

Climax 2300-2100

E U B O E A

Lake Copais

Orchomenos

Gla

Thebes

Ithaca

Haliartos

BOEOTIA

Pottery c. 27th century

GULF OF CORINTH

Eutresis

Tanagra

ATTICA

Isthmus fortified

Corinth

Athens

Shaft-graves c.1500, beehive tombs and palaces 14th century, destroyed 12th

Mycenae

Dendra

SARONIC GULF

Ceo

ARGOLID

Lerna

Tiryns

Asine

Settlement 23rd century, destroyed c.2100

GULF OF ARGOS

Group of Mycenaean centres

PELOPONNESE

Malthi

MESSENIA

LACONIA

Me

Palace, finds of Linear 'B' script; fell in 12th century

Pylos

Elafonisi

Cythera

Satellite and port of Mycenae

Earthquakes c. 1500-1400 raised seaboard

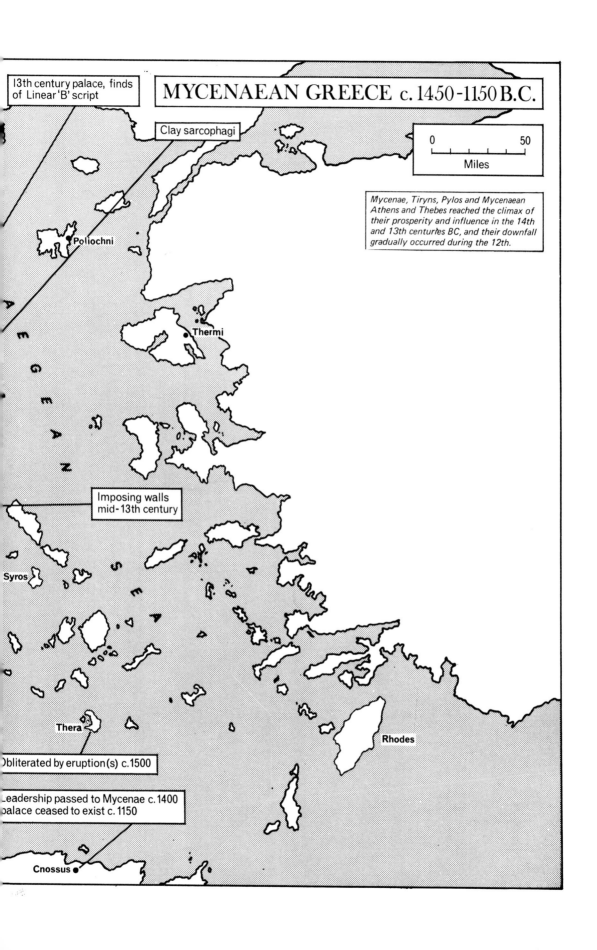

MYCENAEAN GREECE c. 1450-1150 B.C.

13th century palace, finds of Linear 'B' script

Clay sarcophagi

0   50
Miles

Mycenae, Tiryns, Pylos and Mycenaean Athens and Thebes reached the climax of their prosperity and influence in the 14th and 13th centuries BC, and their downfall gradually occurred during the 12th.

Poliochni

A E G E A N

Thermi

Imposing walls mid-13th century

S
E
A

Syros

Thera

Rhodes

Obliterated by eruption(s) c.1500

Leadership passed to Mycenae c.1400 palace ceased to exist c.1150

Cnossus

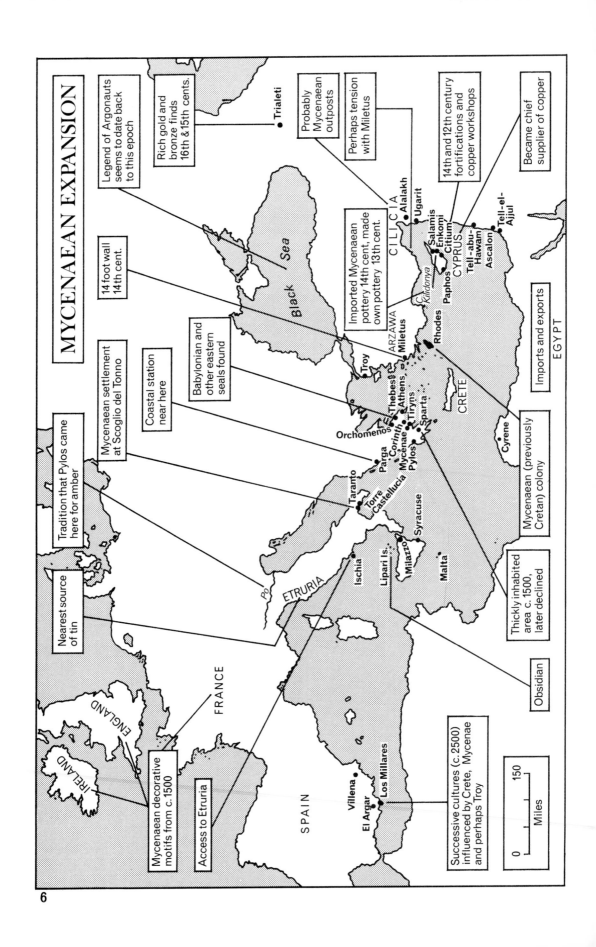

MYCENAEAN EXPANSION

Legend of Argonauts seems to date back to this epoch

Rich gold and bronze finds 16th & 15th cents.

Probably Mycenaean outposts

Perhaps tension with Miletus

14th and 12th century fortifications and copper workshops

Became chief supplier of copper

14 foot wall 14th cent.

Imported Mycenaean pottery 14th cent, made its own pottery 13th cent.

Babylonian and other eastern seals found

Coastal station near here

Mycenaean settlement at Scoglio del Tonno

Imports and exports

Tradition that Pylos came here for amber

Mycenaean decorative motifs from c.1500

Access to Etruria

Nearest source of tin

Mycenaean (previously Cretan) colony

Thickly inhabited area c. 1500, later declined

Obsidian

Successive cultures (c. 2500) influenced by Crete, Mycenae and perhaps Troy

Trialeti

Black Sea

CILICIA
Alalakh
Ugarit
Salamis
Enkomi
Citium
CYPRUS
Paphos
Kition
Tell-abu-Hawam
Ascalon
Tell-el-Ajjul
EGYPT

ARZAWA
Miletus
Rhodes
Troy
Thebes
Athens
Tiryns
Sparta
CRETE
Orchomenos
Corinth
Mycenae
Pylos
Parga
Cyrene

Taranto
Torre Castellucia
Syracuse
Milazzo
Lipari Is.
Malta
Ischia

Po
ETRURIA

FRANCE
ENGLAND
IRELAND

SPAIN
Villena
El Argar
Los Millares

0   150
Miles

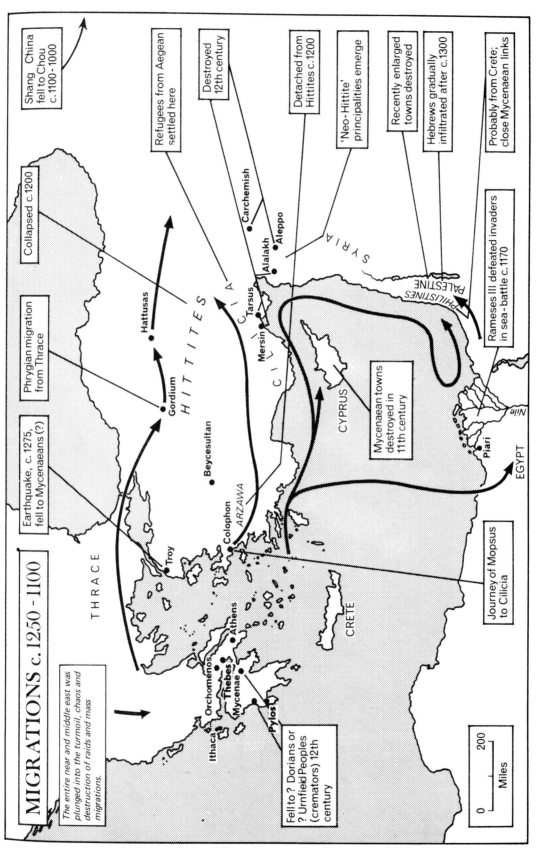

MIGRATIONS c.1250 - 1100

The entire near and middle east was plunged into the turmoil, chaos and destruction of raids and mass migrations.

Shang China fell to Chou c.1100-1000

Refugees from Aegean settled here

Destroyed 12th century

Detached from Hittites c.1200

'Neo-Hittite' principalities emerge

Recently enlarged towns destroyed

Hebrews gradually infiltrated after c.1300

Probably from Crete; close Mycenaean links

Collapsed c.1200

Phrygian migration from Thrace

Earthquake, c.1275, fell to Mycenaeans (?)

Rameses III defeated invaders in sea-battle c.1170

Carchemish

Aleppo

Alalakh

SYRIA

PHILISTINES

PALESTINE

Hattusas

Tarsus

Mersin

C I L I C I A

HITTITES

Gordium

Beycesultan

CYPRUS

Mycenaean towns destroyed in 11th century

Troy

THRACE

Colophon

ARZAWA

Nile

Piari

EGYPT

Journey of Mopsus to Cilicia

CRETE

Athens

Orchomenos

Thebes

Mycenae

Ithaca

Pylos

Fell to ? Dorians or ? Urnfield Peoples (cremators) 12th century

0 ⎯⎯ 200

Miles

7

PHOENICIAN TRADE & COLONISATION

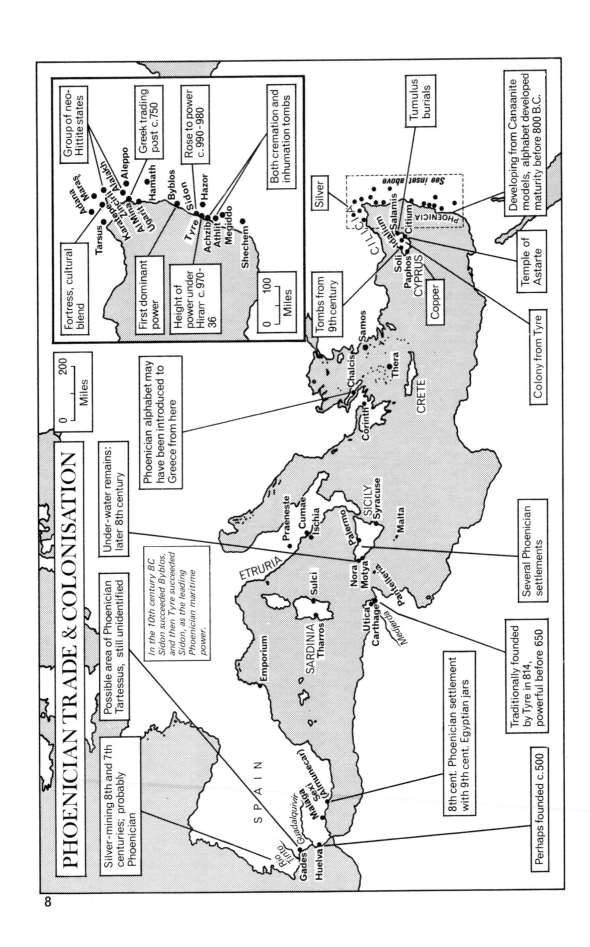

Silver-mining 8th and 7th centuries; probably Phoenician

Possible area of Phoenician Tartessus, still unidentified

Under-water remains: later 8th century

Phoenician alphabet may have been introduced to Greece from here

In the 10th century BC Sidon succeeded Byblos, and then Tyre succeeded Sidon, as the leading Phoenician maritime power.

Group of neo-Hittite states

Greek trading post c. 750

Rose to power c. 990 - 980

Both cremation and inhumation tombs

Fortress, cultural blend

First dominant power

Height of power under Hiram c. 970-36

Tombs from 9th century

Silver

Tumulus burials

Developing from Canaanite models, alphabet developed maturity before 800 B.C.

Temple of Astarte

Copper

Colony from Tyre

Several Phoenician settlements

Traditionally founded by Tyre in 814, powerful before 650

8th cent. Phoenician settlement with 9th cent. Egyptian jars

Perhaps founded c. 500

Adana
Zincirli Alalakh Aleppo
Karatepe
Tarsus
Al Mina Ugarit Hamath
Byblos
Sidon
Tyre Hazor
Achzib
Athlit Megiddo
Shechem

0   100
Miles

0   200
Miles

CILICIA
Soli Salamis
Paphos Citium
CYPRUS
PHOENICIA
See inset above

Chalcis Samos
Thera
Corinth
CRETE

Praeneste
Cumae
Ischia
Palermo
SICILY
Syracuse
Malta

ETRURIA
Nora Motya
Pantelleria

Emporium

SARDINIA
Sulci
Tharros

Utica
Carthage
Medjerda

S P A I N
Guadalquivir
Malaga
Sexi (Almuñecar)
Rio Tinto
Gades
Huelva

8

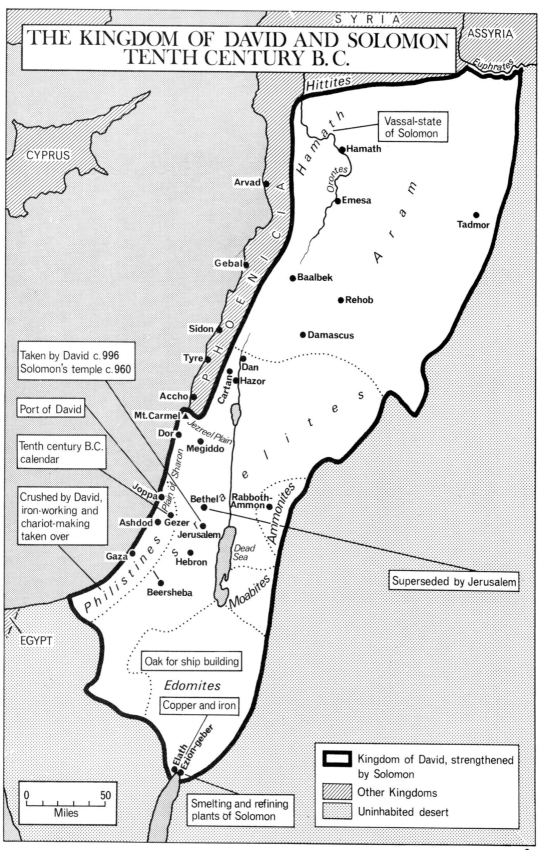

THE KINGDOM OF DAVID AND SOLOMON TENTH CENTURY B.C.

SYRIA

ASSYRIA

Euphrates

Hittites

CYPRUS

Vassal-state of Solomon

Hamath

Arvad

Emesa

Tadmor

Gebal

Baalbek

Rehob

Sidon

Damascus

Tyre

Dan

Taken by David c.996
Solomon's temple c.960

Hazor

Cartan

Accho

Port of David

Mt.Carmel

Dor

Jezreel Plain

Tenth century B.C.
calendar

Megiddo

Joppa

Crushed by David,
iron-working and
chariot-making
taken over

Bethel

Rabboth-
Ammon

Ashdod

Gezer

Jerusalem

Superseded by Jerusalem

Gaza

Hebron

Dead
Sea

Beersheba

Moabites

Oak for ship building

EGYPT

Edomites

Copper and iron

Elath
Ezion-geber

Smelting and refining
plants of Solomon

0   50
Miles

	Kingdom of David, strengthened by Solomon
	Other Kingdoms
	Uninhabited desert

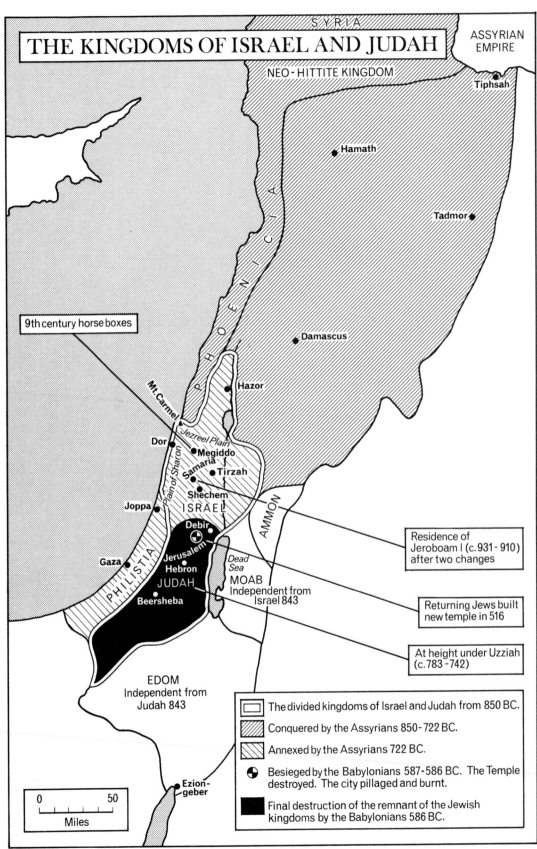

THE KINGDOMS OF ISRAEL AND JUDAH

SYRIA

NEO - HITTITE KINGDOM

ASSYRIAN EMPIRE

Tiphsah

Hamath

Tadmor

P H O E N I C I A

9th century horse boxes

Damascus

Mt. Carmel

Hazor

Jezreel Plain

Dor

Megiddo

Samaria

Tirzah

Plain of Sharon

Shechem

Joppa

ISRAEL

Debir

AMMON

Gaza

Jerusalem

Hebron

Dead Sea

Residence of Jeroboam I (c. 931 - 910) after two changes

JUDAH

MOAB
Independent from Israel 843

Returning Jews built new temple in 516

Beersheba

PHILISTIA

At height under Uzziah (c. 783 - 742)

EDOM
Independent from Judah 843

☐ The divided kingdoms of Israel and Judah from 850 BC.

Conquered by the Assyrians 850 - 722 BC.

Annexed by the Assyrians 722 BC.

⊕ Besieged by the Babylonians 587 - 586 BC. The Temple destroyed. The city pillaged and burnt.

■ Final destruction of the remnant of the Jewish kingdoms by the Babylonians 586 BC.

Ezion-geber

0   50
Miles

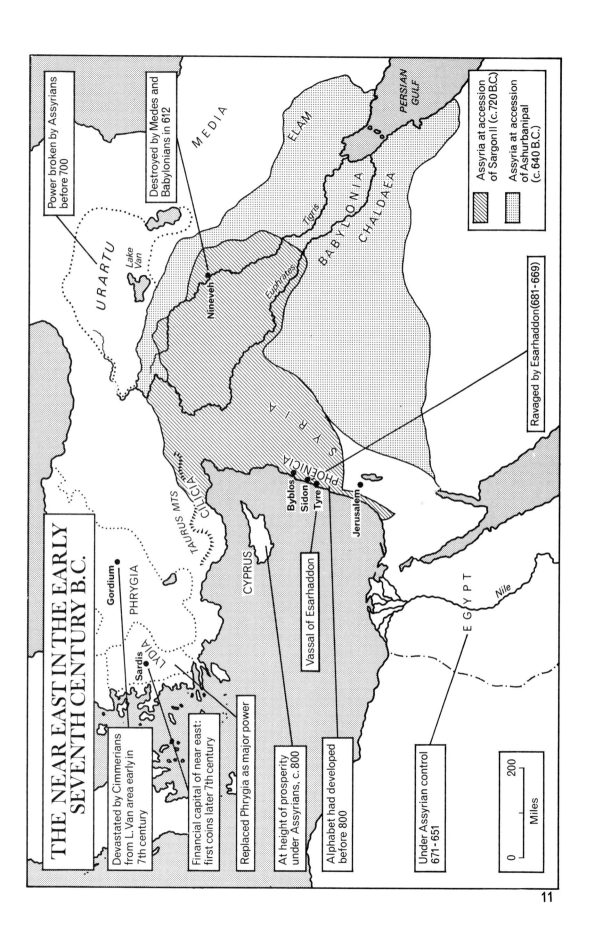

THE NEAR EAST IN THE EARLY SEVENTH CENTURY B.C.

Power broken by Assyrians before 700

Destroyed by Medes and Babylonians in 612

Assyria at accession of Sargon II (c.720 B.C.)

Assyria at accession of Ashurbanipal (c. 640 B.C.)

Ravaged by Esarhaddon (681-669)

Vassal of Esarhaddon

Devastated by Cimmerians from L. Van area early in 7th century

Financial capital of near east: first coins later 7th century

Replaced Phrygia as major power

At height of prosperity under Assyrians, c. 800

Alphabet had developed before 800

Under Assyrian control 671-651

MEDIA

ELAM

PERSIAN GULF

URARTU

Lake Van

Nineveh

Tigris

Euphrates

BABYLONIA

CHALDAEA

SYRIA

TAURUS MTS

CILICIA

PHOENICIA

Byblos

Sidon

Tyre

Jerusalem

CYPRUS

Gordium

PHRYGIA

Sardis

LYDIA

EGYPT

Nile

0   200

Miles

11

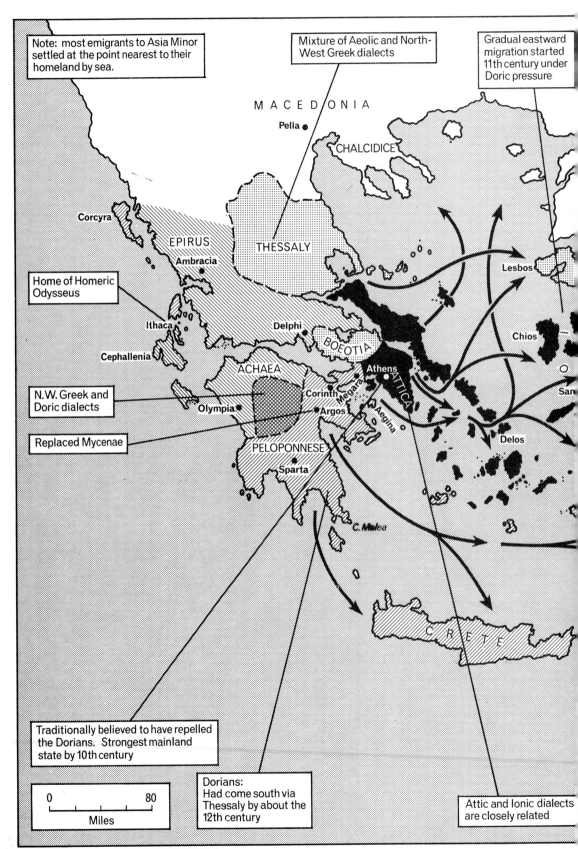

Note: most emigrants to Asia Minor settled at the point nearest to their homeland by sea.

Mixture of Aeolic and North-West Greek dialects

Gradual eastward migration started 11th century under Doric pressure

M A C E D O N I A

Pella ●

CHALCIDICE

Corcyra

EPIRUS

Ambracia

THESSALY

Home of Homeric Odysseus

Ithaca

Delphi

BOEOTIA

Lesbos

Cephallenia

ACHAEA

Chios

N.W. Greek and Doric dialects

Olympia ●

Corinth

Megara

Athens ●

ATTICA

San

Argos

Aegina

Replaced Mycenae

PELOPONNESE

Delos

Sparta ●

C. Malea

C R E T E

Traditionally believed to have repelled the Dorians. Strongest mainland state by 10th century

0   80

Miles

Dorians:
Had come south via Thessaly by about the 12th century

Attic and Ionic dialects are closely related

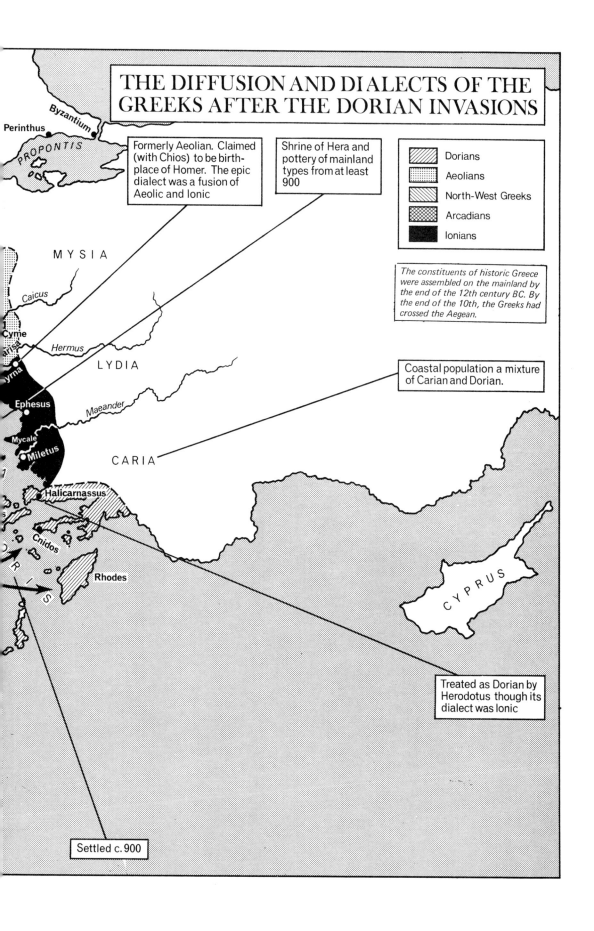

THE DIFFUSION AND DIALECTS OF THE GREEKS AFTER THE DORIAN INVASIONS

Formerly Aeolian. Claimed (with Chios) to be birthplace of Homer. The epic dialect was a fusion of Aeolic and Ionic

Shrine of Hera and pottery of mainland types from at least 900

▨	Dorians
▨	Aeolians
▨	North-West Greeks
▨	Arcadians
■	Ionians

The constituents of historic Greece were assembled on the mainland by the end of the 12th century BC. By the end of the 10th, the Greeks had crossed the Aegean.

Coastal population a mixture of Carian and Dorian.

Treated as Dorian by Herodotus though its dialect was Ionic

Settled c. 900

Perinthus
Byzantium
PROPONTIS

MYSIA
Caicus
Cyme
Hermus
LYDIA
Ephesus
Maeander
Mycale
Miletus
CARIA
Halicarnassus
Cnidos
Rhodes
CYPRUS

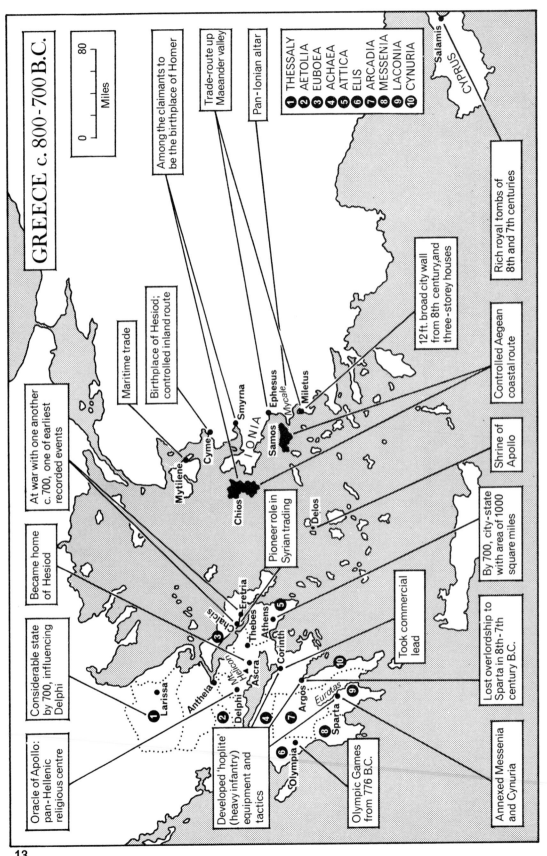

GREECE c. 800-700 B.C.

Miles
0   80

1 THESSALY
2 AETOLIA
3 EUBOEA
4 ACHAEA
5 ATTICA
6 ELIS
7 ARCADIA
8 MESSENIA
9 LACONIA
10 CYNURIA

Among the claimants to be the birthplace of Homer

Trade-route up Maeander valley

Pan-Ionian altar

Maritime trade

Birthplace of Hesiod; controlled inland route

At war with one another c. 700, one of earliest recorded events

Became home of Hesiod

Considerable state by 700, influencing Delphi

Oracle of Apollo: pan-Hellenic religious centre

Developed 'hoplite' (heavy infantry) equipment and tactics

Olympic Games from 776 B.C.

Annexed Messenia and Cynuria

Lost overlordship to Sparta in 8th–7th century B.C.

By 700, city-state with area of 1000 square miles

Took commercial lead

Shrine of Apollo

Controlled Aegean coastal route

Rich royal tombs of 8th and 7th centuries

12 ft. broad city wall from 8th century, and three-storey houses

Pioneer role in Syrian trading

CYPRUS

Salamis

IONIA

Smyrna
Ephesus
Mycale
Miletus
Samos
Cyme
Mytilene
Chios
Delos

Larissa
Chalcis
Eretria
Thebes
Athens
Corinth
Argos
Eurotas
Sparta
Olympia
Anthela
Delphi
Mt. Helicon
Ascra

13

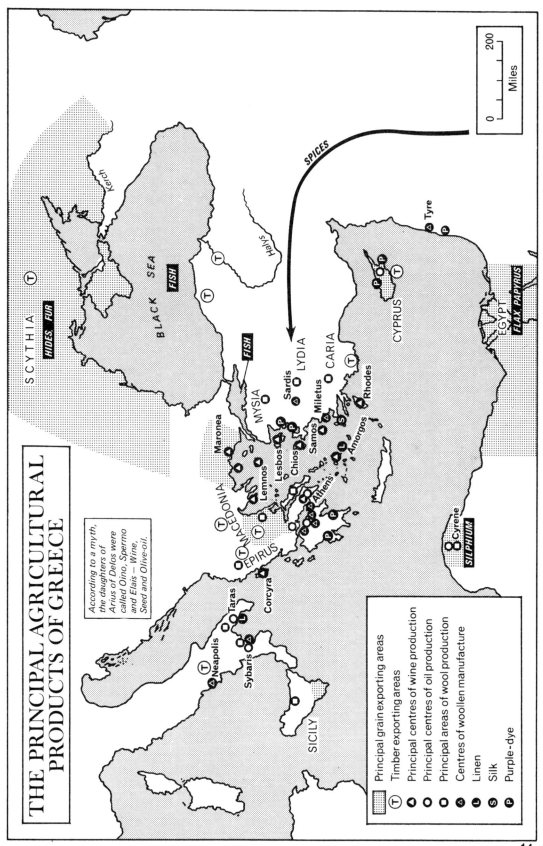

THE PRINCIPAL AGRICULTURAL PRODUCTS OF GREECE

According to a myth, the daughters of Arius of Delos were called Oino, Spermo and Elais — Wine, Seed and Olive-oil.

SPICES

SCYTHIA
HIDES FUR

BLACK SEA

FISH

Kerch

Halys

FISH

Tyre

CYPRUS

EGYPT
FLAX PAPYRUS

MYSIA
Maronea
Lesbos
Lemnos
Chios
MACEDONIA
Samos
Athens
Amorgos
EPIRUS
Sardis
LYDIA
Miletus
CARIA
Rhodes

Corcyra
Taras
Neapolis
Sybaris
SICILY

Cyrene
SILPHIUM

200 Miles
0

Principal grain exporting areas
Timber exporting areas
Principal centres of wine production
Principal centres of oil production
Principal areas of wool production
Centres of woollen manufacture
Linen
Silk
Purple-dye

14

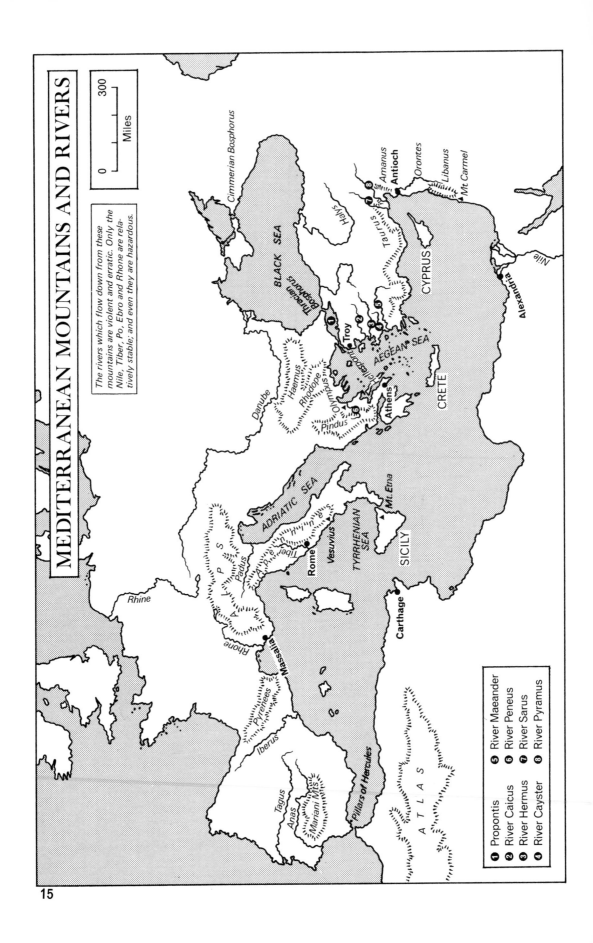

MEDITERRANEAN MOUNTAINS AND RIVERS

0 — 300
Miles

The rivers which flow down from these mountains are violent and erratic. Only the Nile, Tiber, Po, Ebro and Rhone are relatively stable; and even they are hazardous.

Cimmerian Bosphorus

BLACK SEA

Thracian Bosphorus

Danube

Haemus

Rhodope

Pindus

Olympus

Haliacmon

Troy ❶

Halys

Taurus

Amanus ❽ Antioch

Orontes

Libanus

Mt Carmel

CYPRUS

Nile

Alexandria

AEGEAN SEA

Athens

CRETE

❷ ❸

❹

❺

ADRIATIC SEA

A p e n n i n e s

ALPS

Padus

Tiber

Rome

Vesuvius

Mt. Etna

TYRRHENIAN SEA

SICILY

Carthage

Rhine

Rhone

Massilia

Pyrenees

Iberus

Tagus

Anas

Mariani Mts

Pillars of Hercules

A T L A S

❶ Propontis ❺ River Maeander
❷ River Caicus ❻ River Peneus
❸ River Hermus ❼ River Sarus
❹ River Cayster ❽ River Pyramus

15

RAINFALL IN THE MEDITERRANEAN AREA

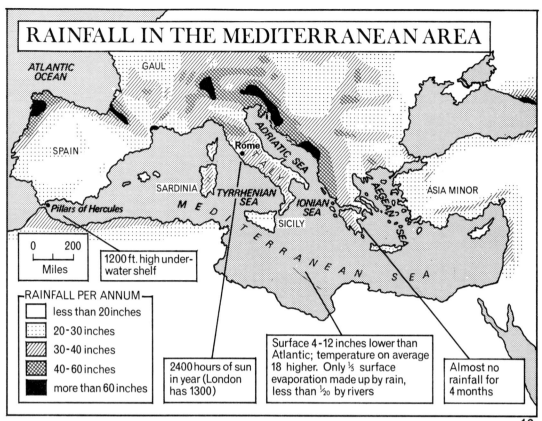

ATLANTIC OCEAN

GAUL

SPAIN

ADRIATIC SEA

Rome

ITALY

SARDINIA

TYRRHENIAN SEA

MEDITERRANEAN SEA

IONIAN SEA

AEGEAN SEA

ASIA MINOR

Pillars of Hercules

SICILY

0   200
Miles

1200 ft. high under-water shelf

RAINFALL PER ANNUM

☐	less than 20 inches
⬚	20-30 inches
▨	30-40 inches
▧	40-60 inches
■	more than 60 inches

2400 hours of sun in year (London has 1300)

Surface 4-12 inches lower than Atlantic; temperature on average 18 higher. Only ⅓ surface evaporation made up by rain, less than ¹⁄₂₀ by rivers

Almost no rainfall for 4 months

16

MINERALS IN THE EASTERN MEDITERRANEAN AREA

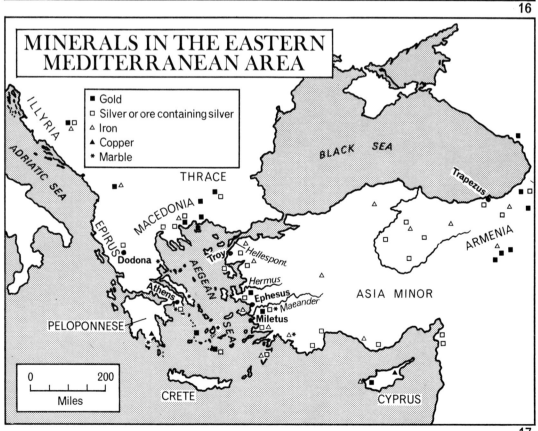

■	Gold
☐	Silver or ore containing silver
△	Iron
▲	Copper
✳	Marble

ILLYRIA

ADRIATIC SEA

THRACE

BLACK SEA

Trapezus

MACEDONIA

EPIRUS

Dodona

Troy

Hellespont

Hermus

ARMENIA

ASIA MINOR

Athens

AEGEAN SEA

Ephesus

Maeander

Miletus

PELOPONNESE

CRETE

CYPRUS

0   200
Miles

17

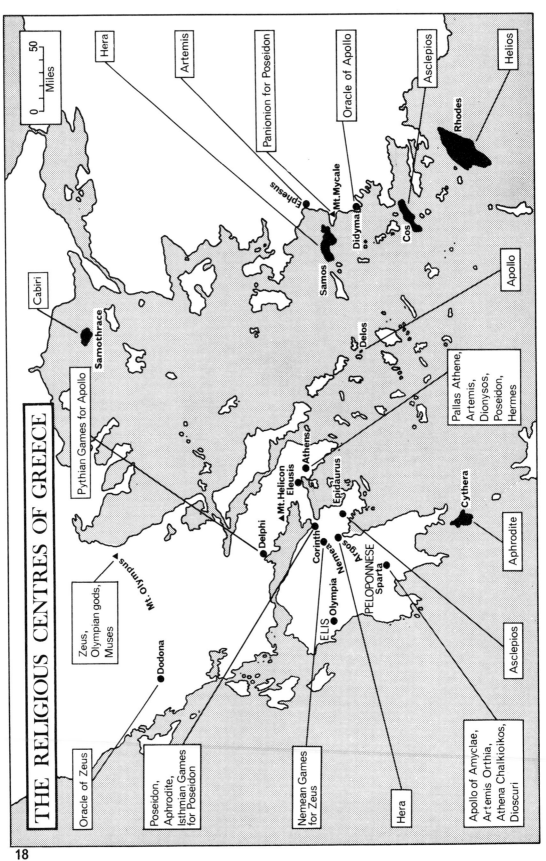

THE RELIGIOUS CENTRES OF GREECE

Miles
0 50

Oracle of Zeus

Zeus, Olympian gods, Muses

▲ Mt. Olympus

● Dodona

Pythian Games for Apollo

Cabiri

Samothrace

Hera

Artemis

Panionion for Poseidon

Oracle of Apollo

Asclepios

Helios

Rhodes

Ephesus ●

Mt. Mycale ▲

Didyma ●

Cos

Apollo

Samos

o. Delos

Pallas Athene, Artemis, Dionysos, Poseidon, Hermes

● Delphi

▲ Mt. Helicon
Eleusis

Athens ●

Epidaurus ●

Corinth ●

Nemea ●

Argos ●

Cythera

Aphrodite

Poseidon, Aphrodite, Isthmian Games for Poseidon

ELIS Olympia ●

PELOPONNESE
Sparta ●

Asclepios

Nemean Games for Zeus

Hera

Apollo of Amyclae, Artemis Orthia, Athena Chalkioikos, Dioscuri

18

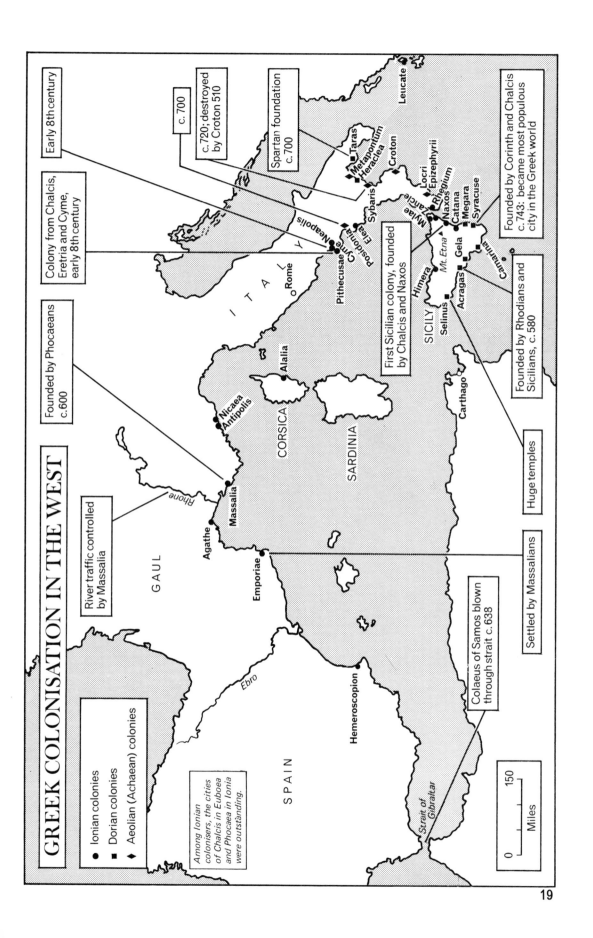

GREEK COLONISATION IN THE WEST

- ● Ionian colonies
- ■ Dorian colonies
- ◆ Aeolian (Achaean) colonies

Among Ionian colonisers, the cities of Chalcis in Euboea and Phocaea in Ionia were outstanding.

Early 8th century

c. 700

c. 720; destroyed by Croton 510

Spartan foundation c. 700

Colony from Chalcis, Eretria and Cyme, early 8th century

Founded by Corinth and Chalcis c. 743: became most populous city in the Greek world

Founded by Phocaeans c. 600

First Sicilian colony, founded by Chalcis and Naxos

Founded by Rhodians and Sicilians, c. 580

River traffic controlled by Massalia

Huge temples

Settled by Massalians

Colaeus of Samos blown through strait c. 638

Leucate

Taras
Metapontum
Heraclea
Croton
Sybaris

Locri Epizephyrii
Rhegium
Mylae
Zancle
Naxos
Catana
Megara
Syracuse

Mt. Etna
Gela
Acragas
Camarina
Selinus
Himera

SICILY

Cyme
Neapolis
Elea
Posidonia
Pithecusae

I T A L Y

○ **Rome**

Rhone

GAUL

Massalia
Nicaea
Antipolis
Agathe
Emporiae

CORSICA
Alalia

SARDINIA

Carthago

Ebro

S P A I N

Hemeroscopion

Strait of Gibraltar

0   150
Miles

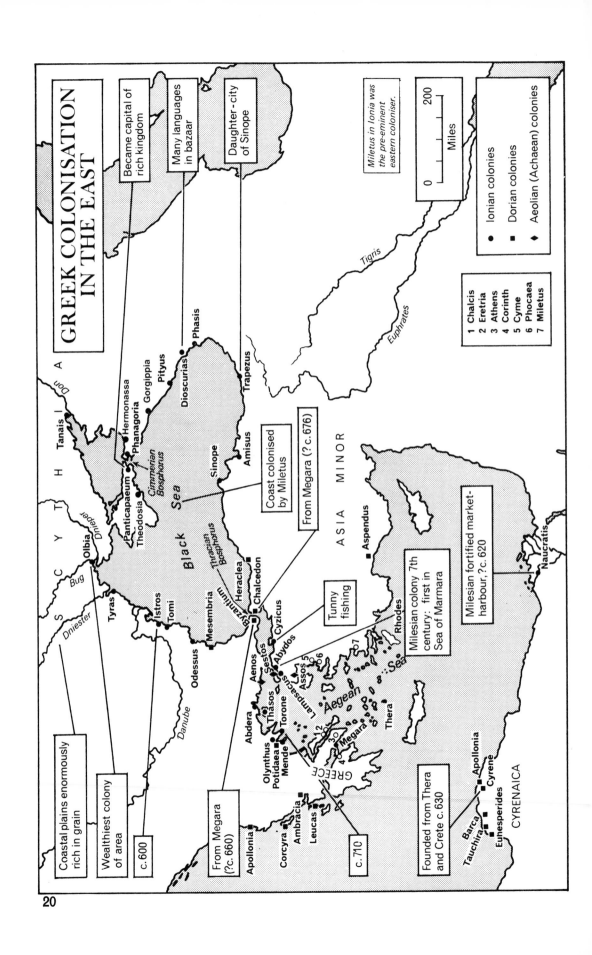

GREEK COLONISATION IN THE EAST

Miletus in Ionia was the pre-eminent eastern coloniser.

0   200
Miles

- ● Ionian colonies
- ■ Dorian colonies
- ◆ Aeolian (Achaean) colonies

1 Chalcis
2 Eretria
3 Athens
4 Corinth
5 Cyme
6 Phocaea
7 Miletus

Became capital of rich kingdom

Many languages in bazaar

Daughter-city of Sinope

Coast colonised by Miletus

From Megara (? c. 676)

Tunny fishing

Milesian colony 7th century: first in Sea of Marmara

Milesian fortified market-harbour, ? c. 620

Coastal plains enormously rich in grain

Wealthiest colony of area

c. 600

From Megara (? c. 660)

c. 710

Founded from Thera and Crete c. 630

Tigris

Euphrates

Phasis

Dioscurias
Pityus
Gorgippia
Hermonassa
Phanagoria
Panticapaeum
Theodosia
Cimmerian Bosphorus
Tanais
Don

Amisus
Sinope
Trapezus

A S I A   M I N O R

Black Sea

Olbia
Dnieper
Bug
Dniester
Tyras
Istros
Tomi
Mesembria
Odessus
Danube
Heraclea
Thracian Bosphorus
Byzantium
Chalcedon
Cyzicus
Abydos
Sestos
Aenos
Abdera
Thasos
Torone
Lampsacus
Assos
5
6
6
7
Rhodes
Aspendus

Aegean Sea

Olynthus
Potidaea
Mende
Megara
Thera
1
2
3
4

GREECE

Apollonia
Corcyra
Ambracia
Leucas

Naucratis

Apollonia
Cyrene
Barca
Tauchira
Eunesperides
CYRENAICA

S C Y T H I A

20

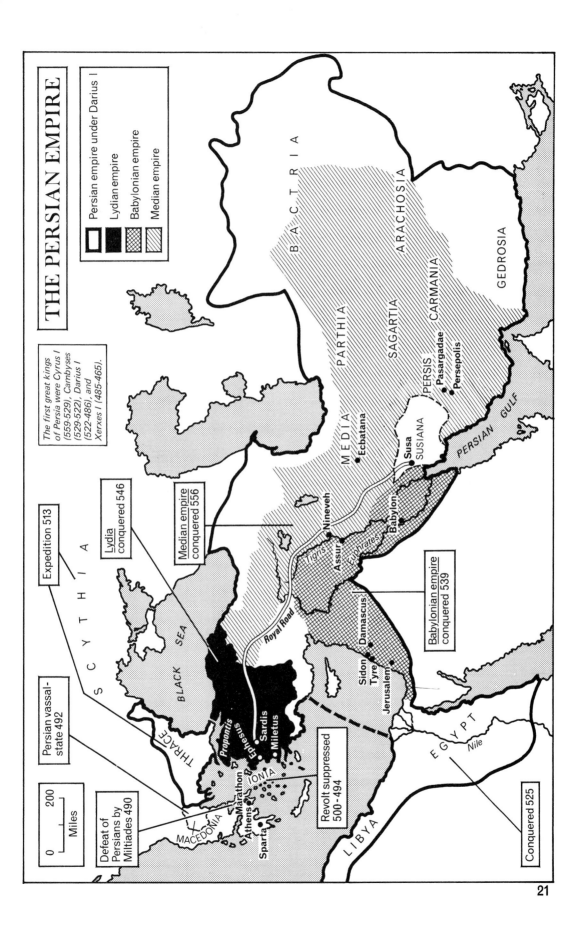

THE PERSIAN EMPIRE

Persian empire under Darius I
Lydian empire
Babylonian empire
Median empire

The first great kings of Persia were Cyrus I (559-529), Cambyses (529-522), Darius I (522-486), and Xerxes I (485-465).

Expedition 513

Lydia conquered 546

Median empire conquered 556

Persian vassal-state 492

Defeat of Persians by Miltiades 490

0   200
Miles

Revolt suppressed 500 - 494

Conquered 525

Babylonian empire conquered 539

BACTRIA

ARACHOSIA

GEDROSIA

PARTHIA

SAGARTIA

CARMANIA

MEDIA

PERSIS

Pasargadae

Persepolis

Ecbatana

Susa

SUSIANA

PERSIAN GULF

Nineveh

Assur

Tigris

Euphrates

Babylon

Damascus

Sidon

Tyre

Jerusalem

EGYPT

Nile

LIBYA

SCYTHIA

BLACK SEA

THRACE

Royal Road

Propontis

Sardis

Ephesus

Miletus

MACEDONIA

Marathon

Athens

IONIA

Sparta

21

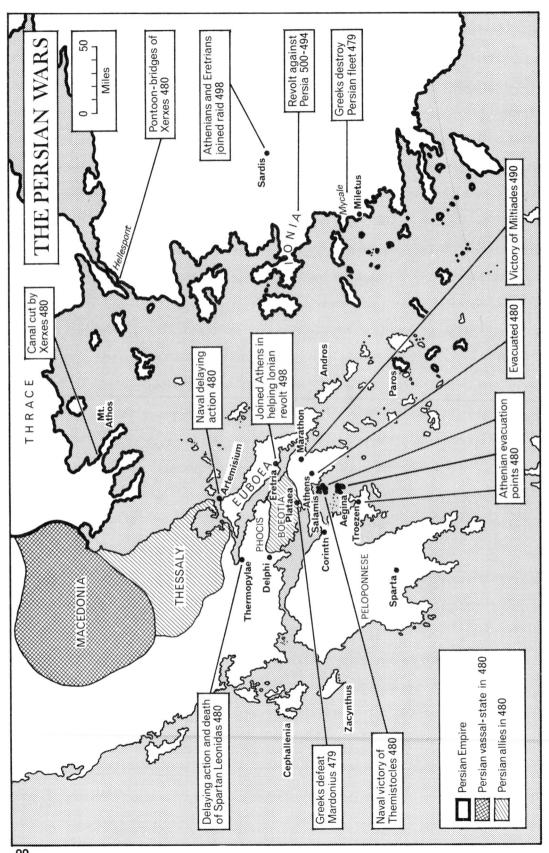

THE PERSIAN WARS

0   50
Miles

Pontoon-bridges of Xerxes 480

Athenians and Eretrians joined raid 498

Revolt against Persia 500-494

Greeks destroy Persian fleet 479

Canal cut by Xerxes 480

Naval delaying action 480

Joined Athens in helping Ionian revolt 498

Victory of Miltiades 490

Evacuated 480

Athenian evacuation points 480

Delaying action and death of Spartan Leonidas 480

Greeks defeat Mardonius 479

Naval victory of Themistocles 480

Sardis

Hellespont

Mt. Athos

THRACE

IONIA

Mycale

Miletus

MACEDONIA

THESSALY

Andros

Paros

Thermopylae

Delphi

PHOCIS

Artemisium

EUBOEA

BOEOTIA

Plataea

Eretria

Marathon

Athens

Salamis

Corinth

Aegina

Troezen

PELOPONNESE

Sparta

Cephallenia

Zacynthus

Persian Empire

Persian vassal-state in 480

Persian allies in 480

22

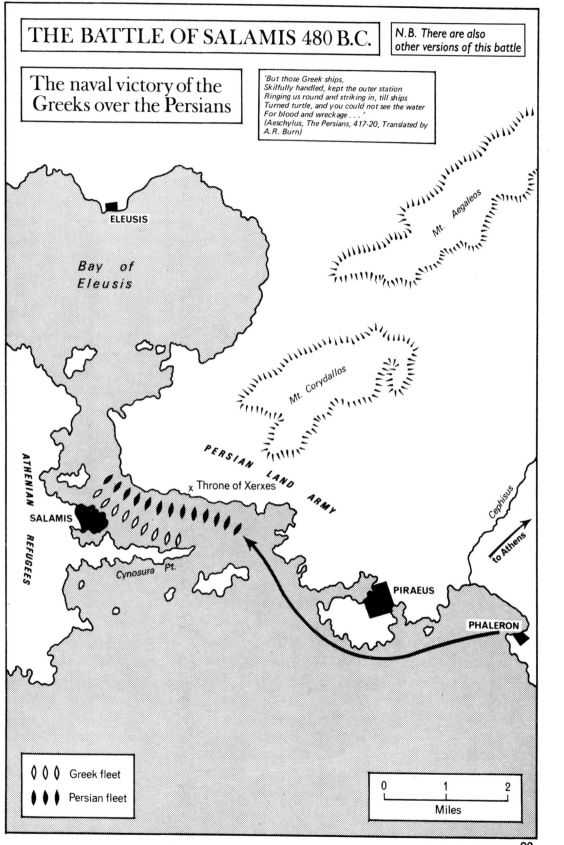

THE BATTLE OF SALAMIS 480 B.C.

N.B. There are also other versions of this battle

The naval victory of the Greeks over the Persians

'But those Greek ships,
Skilfully handled, kept the outer station
Ringing us round and striking in, till ships
Turned turtle, and you could not see the water
For blood and wreckage . . .'
(Aeschylus, The Persians, 417-20, Translated by A.R. Burn)

ELEUSIS

Bay of Eleusis

Mt. Aegaleos

Mt. Corydallos

PERSIAN LAND ARMY

x Throne of Xerxes

Cephisus

to Athens

ATHENIAN REFUGEES

SALAMIS

Cynosura Pt.

PIRAEUS

PHALERON

◊ ◊ ◊ Greek fleet

◆ ◆ ◆ Persian fleet

0   1   2
Miles

23

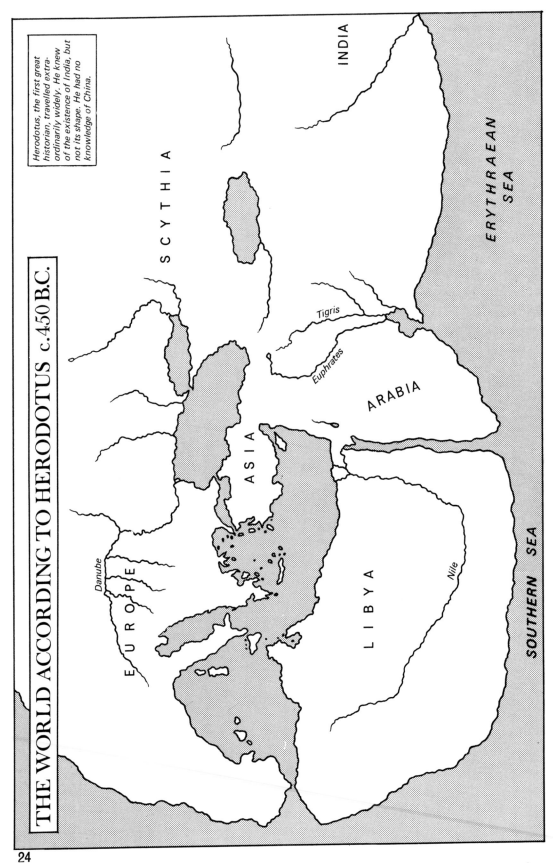

THE WORLD ACCORDING TO HERODOTUS c.450 B.C.

Herodotus, the first great historian, travelled extraordinarily widely. He knew of the existence of India, but not its shape. He had no knowledge of China.

INDIA

SCYTHIA

ERYTHRAEAN SEA

Tigris

Euphrates

ARABIA

ASIA

EUROPE

Danube

LIBYA

Nile

SOUTHERN SEA

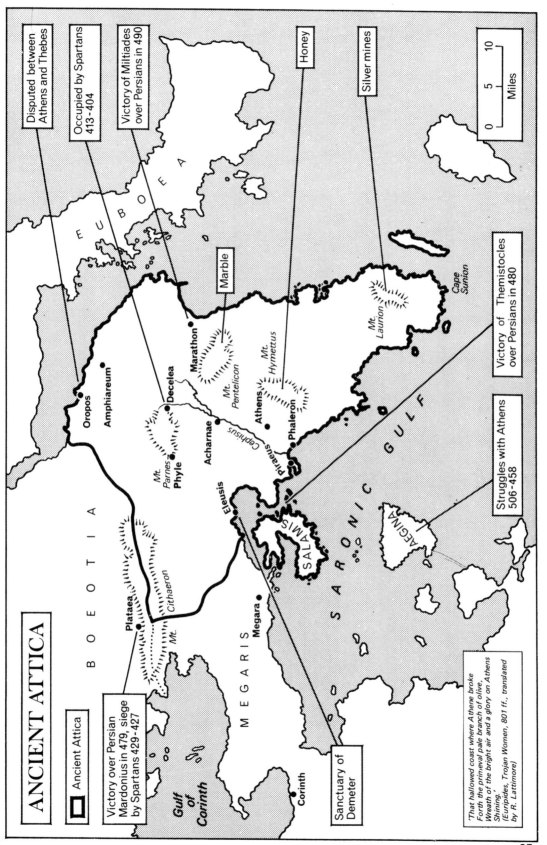

ANCIENT ATTICA

☐ Ancient Attica

Disputed between Athens and Thebes

Occupied by Spartans 413-404

Victory of Miltiades over Persians in 490

Honey

Silver mines

Marble

Victory of Themistocles over Persians in 480

Struggles with Athens 506-458

Victory over Persian Mardonius in 479, siege by Spartans 429-427

Sanctuary of Demeter

'That hallowed coast where Athene broke
Forth the primeval pale branch of olive,
Wreath of the bright air and a glory on Athens
Shining.'
(Euripides, Trojan Women, 801 ff., translated
by R. Lattimore)

EUBOEA

BOEOTIA

B O E O T I A

MEGARIS

M E G A R I S

Gulf of Corinth

Corinth

Megara

Plataea

Mt. Cithaeron

Eleusis

SALAMIS

S A R O N I C   G U L F

AEGINA

Oropos

Amphiareum

Decelea

Mt. Parnes

Phyle

Acharnae

Cephisus

Marathon

Mt. Pentelicon

Athens

Mt. Hymettus

Piraeus

Phaleron

Mt. Laurion

Cape Sunion

Miles
0   5   10

25

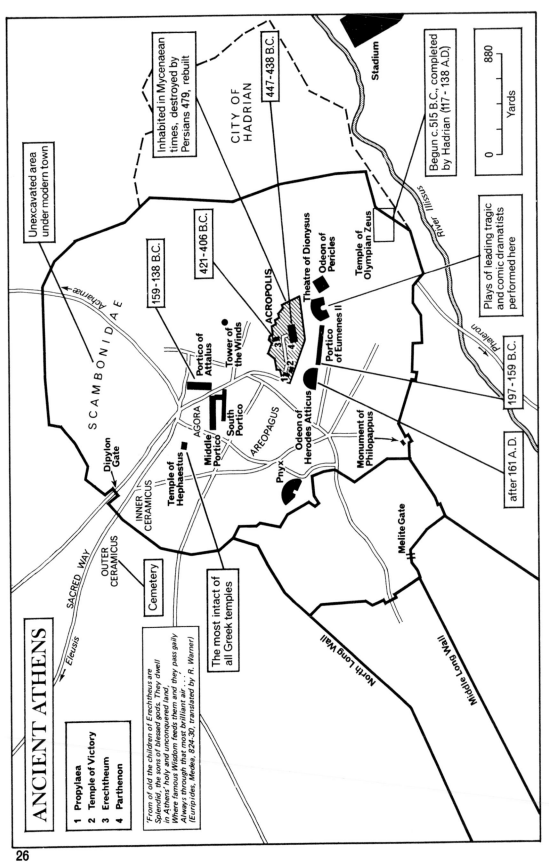

ANCIENT ATHENS

1 Propylaea
2 Temple of Victory
3 Erechtheum
4 Parthenon

'From of old the children of Erechtheus are
Splendid, the sons of blessed gods. They dwell
in Athens' holy and unconquered land,
Where famous Wisdom feeds them and they pass gaily
Always through that most brilliant air ...'.
(Euripides, Medea, 824-30, translated by R. Warner.)

Cemetery

The most intact of
all Greek temples

Unexcavated area
under modern town

Inhabited in Mycenaean
times, destroyed by
Persians 479, rebuilt

447 - 438 B.C.

159 - 138 B.C.

421 - 406 B.C.

CITY OF HADRIAN

Begun c. 515 B.C., completed
by Hadrian (117 - 138 A.D.)

0   880

Yards

Plays of leading tragic
and comic dramatists
performed here

197 - 159 B.C.

after 161 A.D.

SCAMBONIDAE

Acharnae

SACRED WAY

Eleusis

Dipylon
Gate

INNER
CERAMICUS

OUTER
CERAMICUS

Temple of
Hephaestus

AGORA

Portico of
Attalus

Tower of
the Winds

South
Portico

Middle
Portico

AREOPAGUS

Pnyx

Odeon of
Herodes Atticus

Monument of
Philopappus

Melite Gate

North Long Wall

Middle Long Wall

ACROPOLIS

Theatre of Dionysus

Odeon of Pericles

Portico
of Eumenes II

Temple of
Olympian Zeus

Stadium

River Illissus

Phaleron

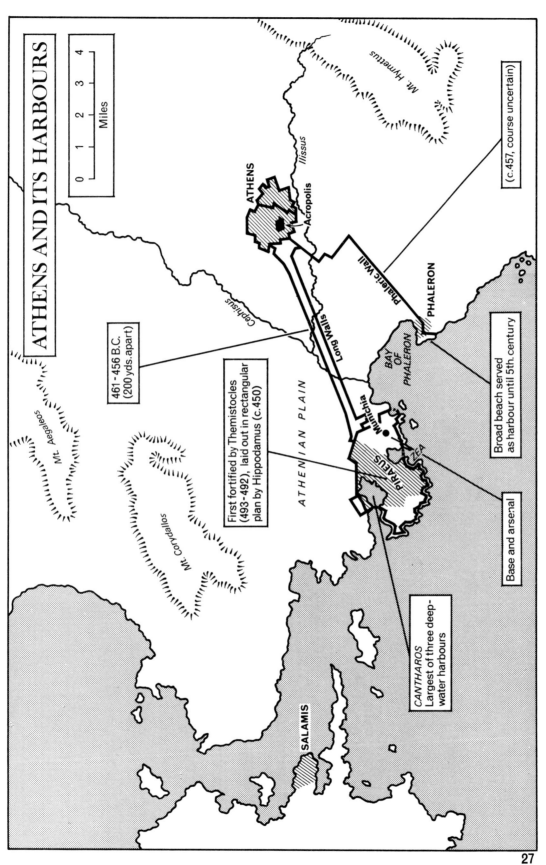

ATHENS AND ITS HARBOURS

Miles
0 1 2 3 4

Mt. Aegaleos

Mt. Corydallos

ATHENIAN PLAIN

Cephisus

ATHENS

Acropolis

Ilissus

Mt. Hymettus

461 - 456 B.C.
(200 yds. apart)

First fortified by Themistocles
(493-492), laid out in rectangular
plan by Hippodamus (c.450)

Long Walls

Phaleric Wall

PHALERON

(c.457, course uncertain)

Munichia

PIRAEUS

ZEA

BAY
OF
PHALERON

Broad beach served
as harbour until 5th. century

Base and arsenal

CANTHAROS
Largest of three deep-
water harbours

SALAMIS

27

THE IMPERIALISM OF FIFTH CENTURY ATHENS

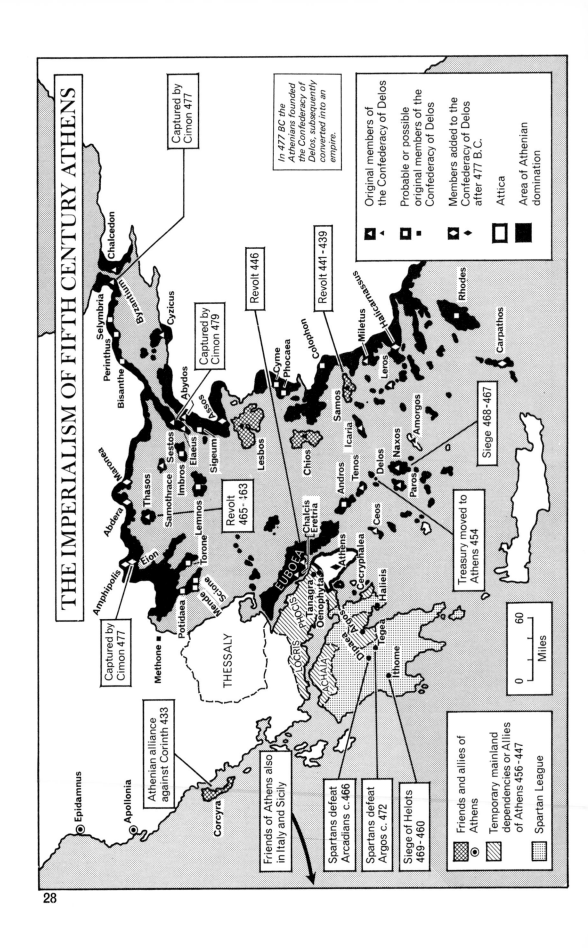

In 477 BC the Athenians founded the Confederacy of Delos, subsequently converted into an empire.

◁ ◀	Original members of the Confederacy of Delos	
☐ ■	Probable or possible original members of the Confederacy of Delos	
◇ ◆	Members added to the Confederacy of Delos after 477 B.C.	
☐	Attica	
■	Area of Athenian domination	

Captured by Cimon 477

Revolt 446

Revolt 441 - 439

Captured by Cimon 479

Siege 468 - 467

Treasury moved to Athens 454

Revolt 465 - 463

Captured by Cimon 477

Athenian alliance against Corinth 433

Friends of Athens also in Italy and Sicily

Spartans defeat Arcadians c.466

Spartans defeat Argos c. 472

Siege of Helots 469 - 460

▨ ◉	Friends and allies of Athens
▨	Temporary mainland dependencies or Allies of Athens 456 - 447
▦	Spartan League

0   60
Miles

28

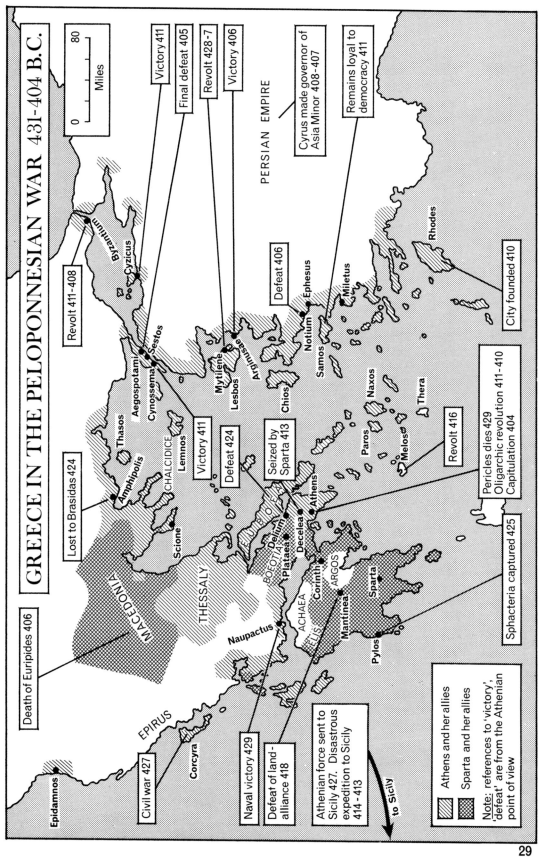

GREECE IN THE PELOPONNESIAN WAR 431–404 B.C.

0 80 Miles

Victory 411
Final defeat 405
Revolt 428–7
Victory 406

PERSIAN EMPIRE

Cyrus made governor of Asia Minor 408–407
Remains loyal to democracy 411

Revolt 411–408
Byzantium
Cyzicus
Sestos
Aegospotami
Cynossema
Thasos
CHALCIDICE
Lemnos
Amphipolis
Scione
Death of Euripides 406
Lost to Brasidas 424
MACEDONIA
THESSALY

Victory 411
Defeat 424
Mytilene
Lesbos
Arginusae
Chios
Seized by Sparta 413
Defeat 406
Notium
Ephesus
Miletus
Samos
Paros Naxos
Melos
Thera
Rhodes

City founded 410
Revolt 416

EUBOEA
BOEOTIA
Delium
Plataea
Decelea
Athens
Corinth
ARGOS
Mantinea
Sparta

Naupactus
ACHAEA
ELIS
Pylos
Sphacteria captured 425
Pericles dies 429
Oligarchic revolution 411–410
Capitulation 404

Civil war 427
Corcyra
EPIRUS
Epidamnos

Naval victory 429
Defeat of land-alliance 418
Athenian force sent to Sicily 427. Disastrous expedition to Sicily 414–413

to Sicily

Athens and her allies
Sparta and her allies
Note: references to 'victory', 'defeat' are from the Athenian point of view

29

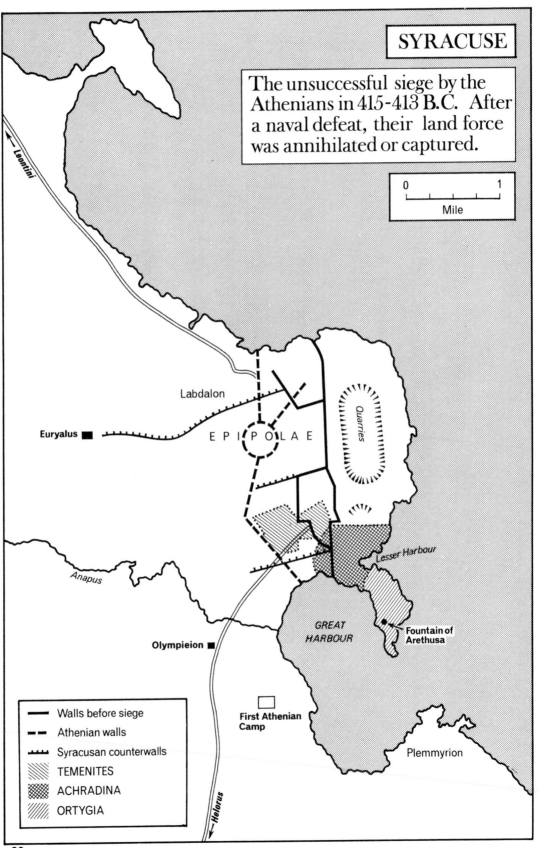

SYRACUSE

The unsuccessful siege by the Athenians in 415-413 B.C. After a naval defeat, their land force was annihilated or captured.

0   1
Mile

Leontini

Labdalon

Euryalus ■

E P I P O L A E

Quarries

Anapus

Lesser Harbour

Olympieion ■

GREAT
HARBOUR

Fountain of
Arethusa

First Athenian
Camp

Plemmyrion

Helorus

Walls before siege
Athenian walls
Syracusan counterwalls
TEMENITES
ACHRADINA
ORTYGIA

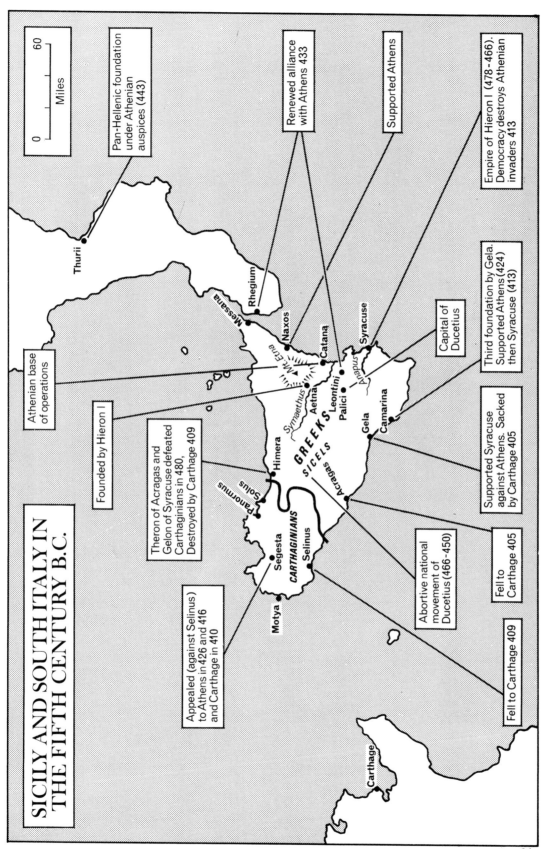

SICILY AND SOUTH ITALY IN THE FIFTH CENTURY B.C.

Miles
0   60

Pan-Hellenic foundation under Athenian auspices (443)

Renewed alliance with Athens 433

Supported Athens

Empire of Hieron I (478–466). Democracy destroys Athenian invaders 413

Athenian base of operations

Founded by Hieron I

Theron of Acragas and Gelon of Syracuse defeated Carthaginians in 480, Destroyed by Carthage 409

Capital of Ducetius

Third foundation by Gela. Supported Athens (424) then Syracuse (413)

Supported Syracuse against Athens. Sacked by Carthage 405

Fell to Carthage 405

Abortive national movement of Ducetius (466–450)

Fell to Carthage 409

Appealed (against Selinus) to Athens in 426 and 416 and Carthage in 410

Thurii

Rhegium

Messana

Naxos

Catana

Syracuse

Mt. Etna

Symaethus

Aetna

Leontini

Palici

Anapus

GREEKS

SICELS

Camarina

Gela

Acragas

Himera

Solus

Panormus

CARTHAGINIANS

Selinus

Segesta

Motya

Carthage

31

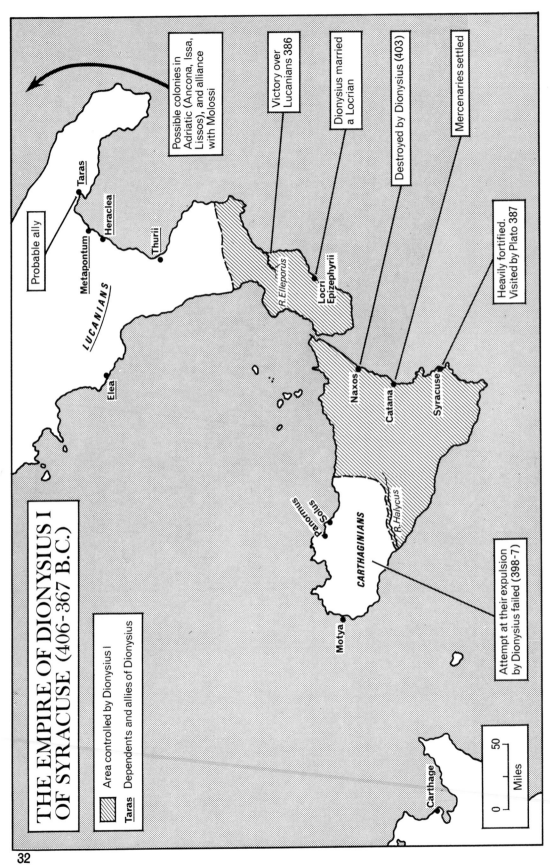

THE EMPIRE OF DIONYSIUS I OF SYRACUSE (406-367 B.C.)

Area controlled by Dionysius I

Taras Dependents and allies of Dionysius

Probable ally

Possible colonies in Adriatic (Ancona, Issa, Lissos), and alliance with Molossi

Victory over Lucanians 386

Dionysius married a Locrian

Destroyed by Dionysius (403)

Mercenaries settled

Heavily fortified. Visited by Plato 387

Attempt at their expulsion by Dionysius failed (398-7)

Taras

Heraclea

Metapontum

Thurii

LUCANIANS

Elea

R.Elleporus

Locri Epizephyrii

Naxos

Catana

Syracuse

Solus

Panormus

CARTHAGINIANS

R. Halycus

Motya

Carthage

0   50

Miles

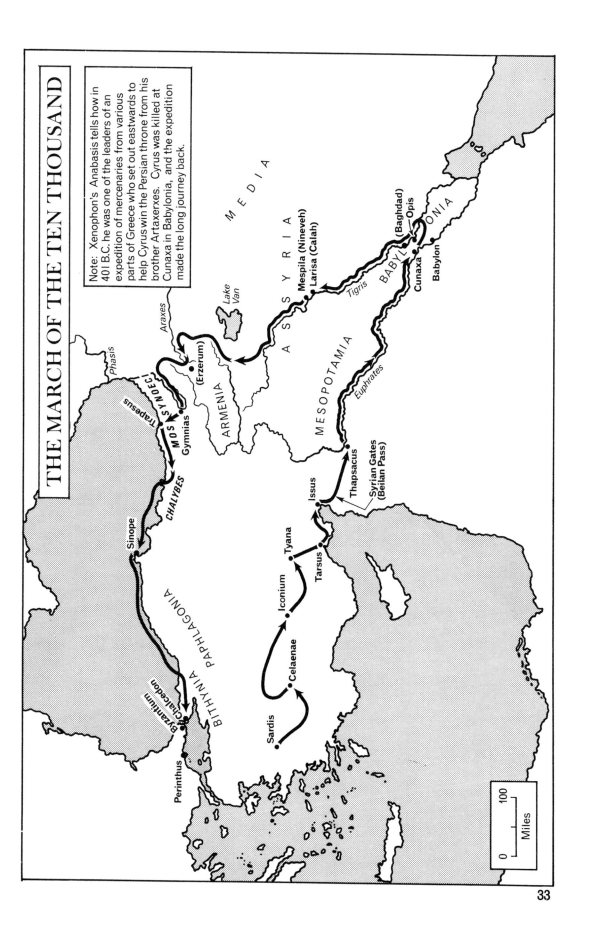

THE MARCH OF THE TEN THOUSAND

Note: Xenophon's Anabasis tells how in 401 B.C. he was one of the leaders of an expedition of mercenaries from various parts of Greece who set out eastwards to help Cyrus win the Persian throne from his brother Artaxerxes. Cyrus was killed at Cunaxa in Babylonia, and the expedition made the long journey back.

MEDIA

ASSYRIA

Lake Van

Araxes

Phasis

MOS SYNOECI

Trapesus

Gymnias

CHALYBES

Sinope

ARMENIA

(Erzerum)

MESOPOTAMIA

Euphrates

Tigris

Mespila (Nineveh)
Larisa (Calah)

BABYL ONIA

(Baghdad)
Opis

Cunaxa

Babylon

Thapsacus

Issus

Syrian Gates
(Beilan Pass)

Tyana

Tarsus

Iconium

Celaenae

Sardis

BITHYNIA PAPHLAGONIA

Byzantium
Chalcedon

Perinthus

0   100
Miles

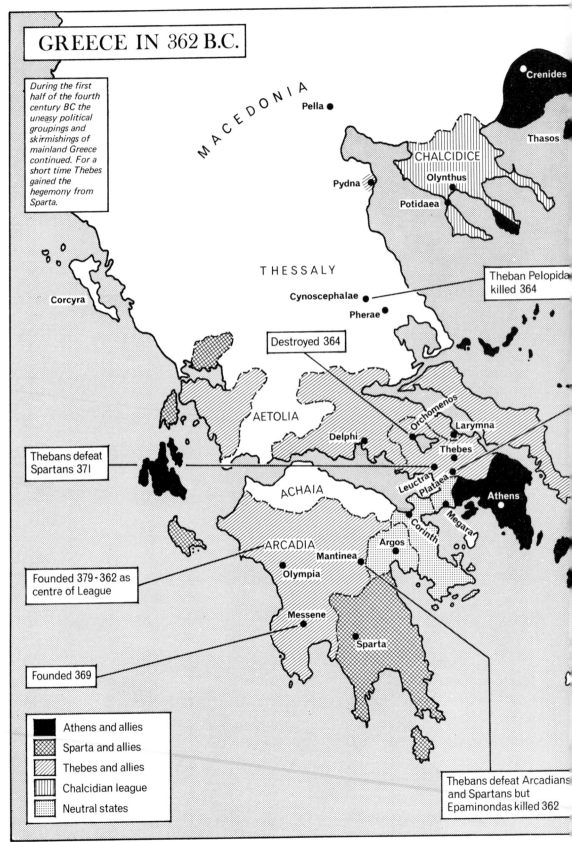

GREECE IN 362 B.C.

During the first half of the fourth century BC the uneasy political groupings and skirmishings of mainland Greece continued. For a short time Thebes gained the hegemony from Sparta.

MACEDONIA

Crenides

Pella

Thasos

CHALCIDICE

Olynthus

Pydna

Potidaea

THESSALY

Corcyra

Cynoscephalae

Theban Pelopida[s]
killed 364

Pherae

Destroyed 364

AETOLIA

Orchomenos

Larymna

Delphi

Thebes

Thebans defeat
Spartans 371

Leuctra

Plataea

Athens

ACHAIA

Megara

Corinth

ARCADIA

Argos

Mantinea

Founded 379-362 as
centre of League

Olympia

Messene

Founded 369

Sparta

Thebans defeat Arcadians
and Spartans but
Epaminondas killed 362

■	Athens and allies
▨	Sparta and allies
▨	Thebes and allies
▥	Chalcidian league
▦	Neutral states

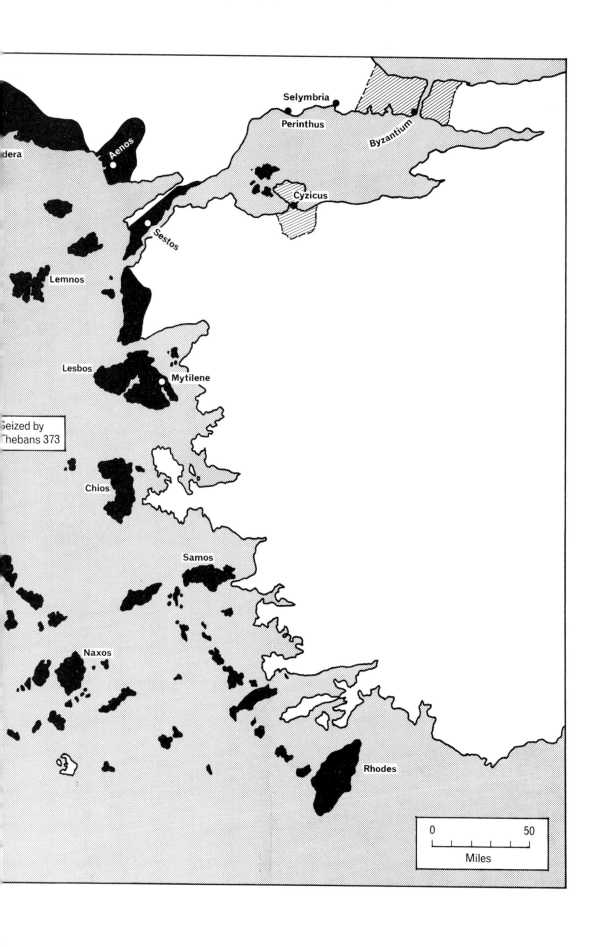

Selymbria

Perinthus

Byzantium

Aenos

dera

Cyzicus

Sestos

Lemnos

Lesbos

Mytilene

Seized by
Thebans 373

Chios

Samos

Naxos

Rhodes

0   50

Miles

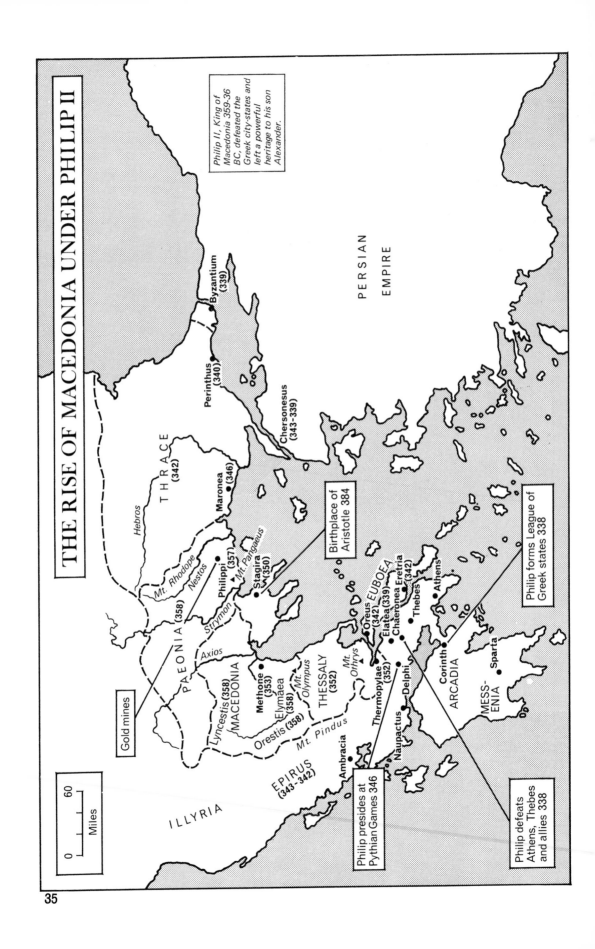

THE RISE OF MACEDONIA UNDER PHILIP II

Philip II, King of Macedonia 359-36 BC, defeated the Greek city-states and left a powerful heritage to his son Alexander.

PERSIAN EMPIRE

Byzantium (339)

Perinthus (340)

Chersonesus (343-339)

THRACE (342)

Maronea (346)

Hebros

Mt. Rhodope

Nestos

Mt. Pangaeus

Philippi (357)

Stagira (350)

Birthplace of Aristotle 384

EUBOEA

Oreus (342)

Elatea (339)

Eretria (342)

Chaeronea (342)

Thebes

Athens

Philip forms League of Greek states 338

Gold mines

PAEONIA (358)

Strymon

Axios

Lyncestis (358)

MACEDONIA

Methone (353)

Elymaea (358)

Mt. Olympus

Orestis (358)

THESSALY (352)

Mt. Othrys

Thermopylae (352)

Delphi

Naupactus

Corinth

ARCADIA

Sparta

MESS-
ENIA

Philip defeats Athens, Thebes and allies 338

Mt. Pindus

EPIRUS (343-342)

Ambracia

Philip presides at Pythian Games 346

ILLYRIA

0   60
Miles

35

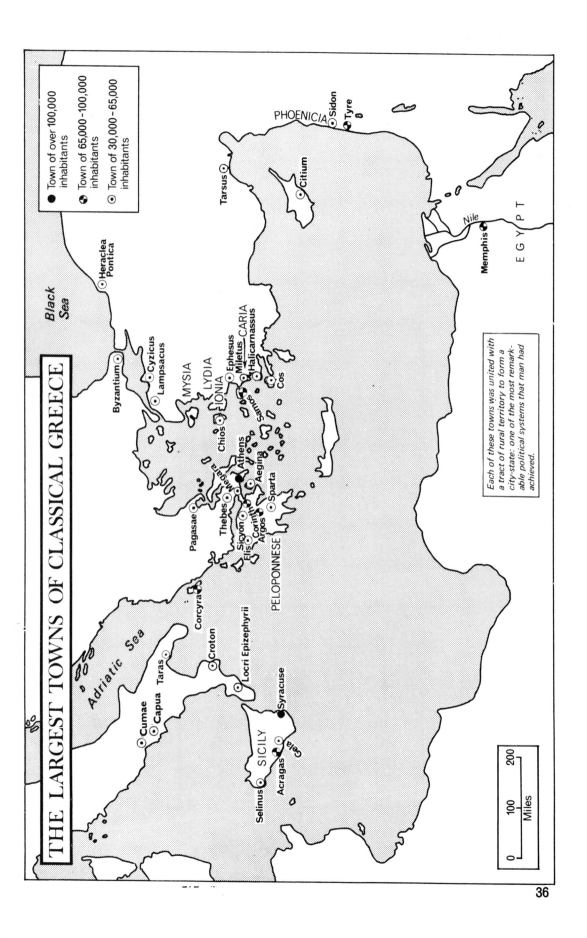

THE LARGEST TOWNS OF CLASSICAL GREECE

Town of over 100,000 inhabitants

Town of 65,000 - 100,000 inhabitants

Town of 30,000 - 65,000 inhabitants

Black Sea

Byzantium

Heraclea Pontica

Cyzicus
Lampsacus

MYSIA
LYDIA
IONIA
Chios
Ephesus
Miletus CARIA
Halicarnassus
Cos
Samos

Tarsus

Citium

PHOENICIA Sidon
Tyre

Nile

Memphis

E G Y P T

Pagasae

Thebes
Megara
Athens
Aegina
Sparta
Sicyon
Elis Corinth
Argos

PELOPONNESE

Corcyra

Croton

Locri Epizephyrii

Taras
Capua
Cumae

Syracuse

SICILY
Gela
Acragas
Selinus

Adriatic Sea

Each of these towns was united with a tract of rural territory to form a city-state: one of the most remarkable political systems that man had achieved.

0   100   200
Miles

36

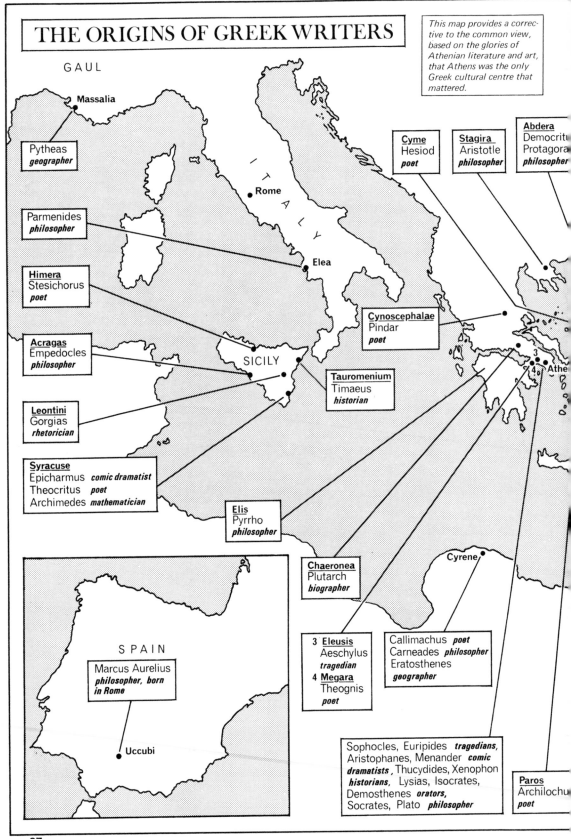

THE ORIGINS OF GREEK WRITERS

This map provides a corrective to the common view, based on the glories of Athenian literature and art, that Athens was the only Greek cultural centre that mattered.

GAUL

Massalia

Pytheas
geographer

Parmenides
philosopher

Himera
Stesichorus
poet

Acragas
Empedocles
philosopher

Leontini
Gorgias
rhetorician

Syracuse
Epicharmus   *comic dramatist*
Theocritus   *poet*
Archimedes   *mathematician*

Rome

Elea

SICILY

Cyme
Hesiod
poet

Stagira
Aristotle
philosopher

Abdera
Democritu
Protagora
philosopher

Cynoscephalae
Pindar
poet

Tauromenium
Timaeus
historian

Athe

Elis
Pyrrho
philosopher

Chaeronea
Plutarch
biographer

Cyrene

SPAIN

Marcus Aurelius
philosopher, born in Rome

Uccubi

3 **Eleusis**
Aeschylus
tragedian
4 **Megara**
Theognis
poet

Callimachus *poet*
Carneades *philosopher*
Eratosthenes
geographer

Sophocles, Euripides *tragedians*,
Aristophanes, Menander *comic dramatists*, Thucydides, Xenophon
historians, Lysias, Isocrates,
Demosthenes *orators*,
Socrates, Plato *philosopher*

Paros
Archilochu
poet

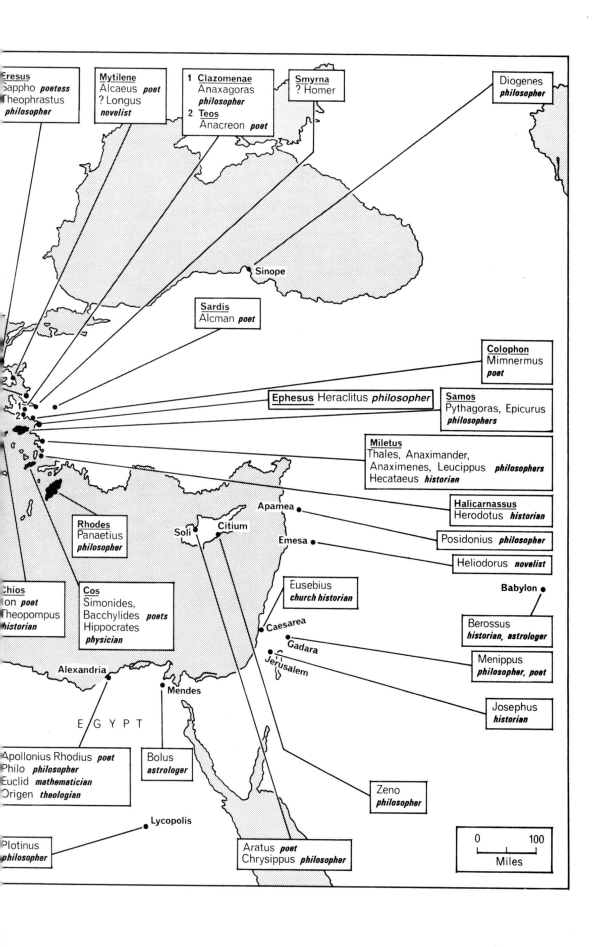

Eresus
Sappho *poetess*
Theophrastus
philosopher

Mytilene
Alcaeus *poet*
? Longus *novelist*

1 **Clazomenae**
Anaxagoras
philosopher
2 **Teos**
Anacreon *poet*

Smyrna
? Homer

Diogenes
philosopher

Sinope

Sardis
Alcman *poet*

Colophon
Mimnermus
poet

Ephesus Heraclitus *philosopher*

Samos
Pythagoras, Epicurus
philosophers

Miletus
Thales, Anaximander,
Anaximenes, Leucippus *philosophers*
Hecataeus *historian*

Apamea

Halicarnassus
Herodotus *historian*

Rhodes
Panaetius
philosopher

Soli

Citium

Emesa

Posidonius *philosopher*

Heliodorus *novelist*

Chios
Ion *poet*
Theopompus
historian

Cos
Simonides,
Bacchylides *poets*
Hippocrates
physician

Eusebius
church historian

Babylon

Caesarea

Gadara

Jerusalem

Berossus
historian, astrologer

Menippus
philosopher, poet

Alexandria

Mendes

E G Y P T

Josephus
historian

Apollonius Rhodius *poet*
Philo *philosopher*
Euclid *mathematician*
Origen *theologian*

Bolus
astrologer

Zeno
philosopher

Lycopolis

Plotinus
philosopher

Aratus *poet*
Chrysippus *philosopher*

0   100
Miles

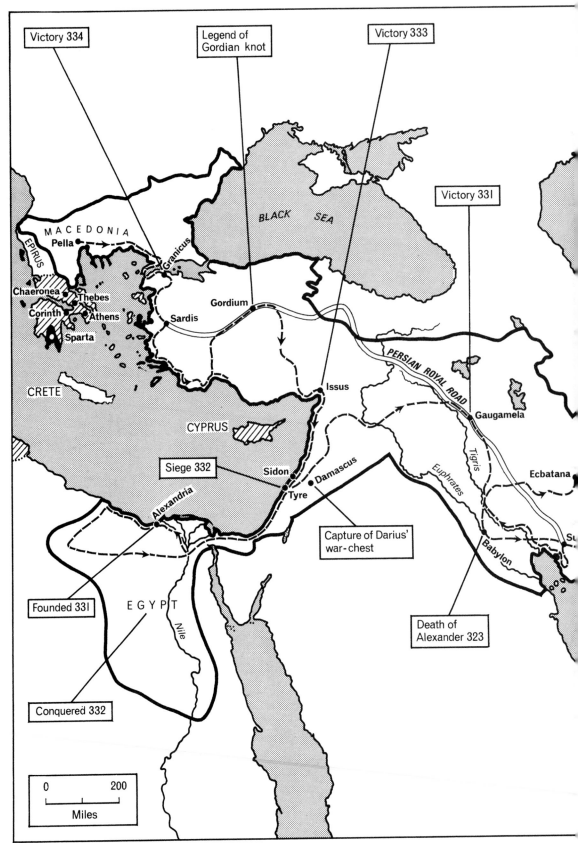

Victory 334

Legend of
Gordian knot

Victory 333

Victory 331

BLACK   SEA

MACEDONIA

EPIRUS

Pella

Chaeronea

Thebes

Corinth

Athens

Sparta

CRETE

Granicus

Gordium

Sardis

Issus

CYPRUS

Siege 332

Sidon

Damascus

Tyre

Alexandria

Capture of Darius'
war-chest

Founded 331

EGYPT

Nile

PERSIAN ROYAL ROAD

Gaugamela

Tigris

Ecbatana

Euphrates

Babylon

Su

Death of
Alexander 323

Conquered 332

0   200

Miles

THE CONQUESTS OF ALEXANDER THE GREAT

Alexander III of Macedonia succeeded his father Philip II in 336, and, after conquests that utterly changed the world, died at Babylon in 323.

☐	Empire of Alexander the Great
▨	Dependent states
■	Independent states
– – →	Routes of Alexander the Great

Conquered 328

Darius murdered 330

CASPIAN SEA

SOGDIANA

Alexandria Eschate

PUNJAB

Alexandria (Merv)

Bactra (Balkh)

BACTRIA

Alexandria

Taxila

Damghan

PARTHIA

Alexandria (Herat)

Alexandria (Ghazni)

Bucephala

Indus

Hydaspes

Occupied 331

Alexandria (Kandahar)

Persepolis

Alexandria

GEDROSIA

PERSIAN GULF

Victory over Indian king Porus 326

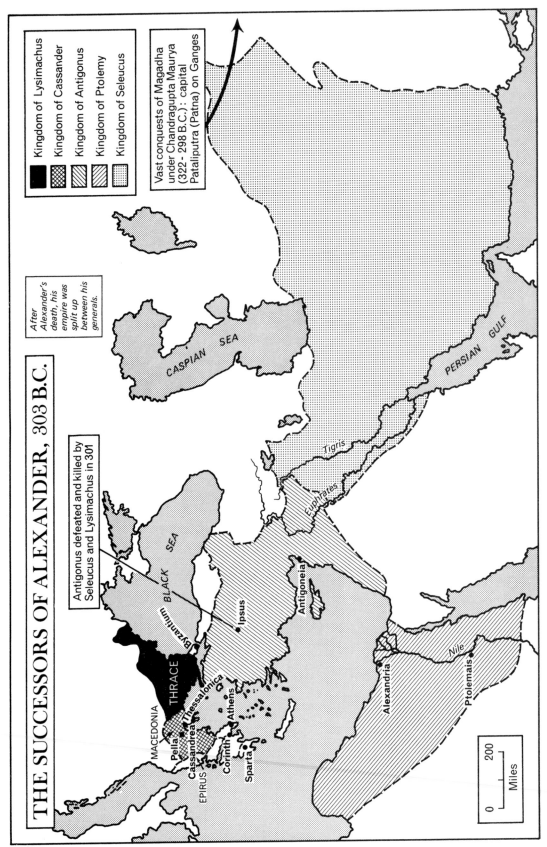

THE SUCCESSORS OF ALEXANDER, 303 B.C.

Legend

- Kingdom of Lysimachus
- Kingdom of Cassander
- Kingdom of Antigonus
- Kingdom of Ptolemy
- Kingdom of Seleucus

Vast conquests of Magadha under Chandragupta Maurya (322 - 298 B.C.): capital Pataliputra (Patna) on Ganges

After Alexander's death, his empire was split up between his generals.

Antigonus defeated and killed by Seleucus and Lysimachus in 301

CASPIAN SEA

BLACK SEA

Byzantium

THRACE

MACEDONIA

Pella

Cassandrea

Thessalonica

EPIRUS

Corinth

Athens

Sparta

Ipsus

Antigoneia

Euphrates

Tigris

PERSIAN GULF

Alexandria

Nile

Ptolemais

0   200
Miles

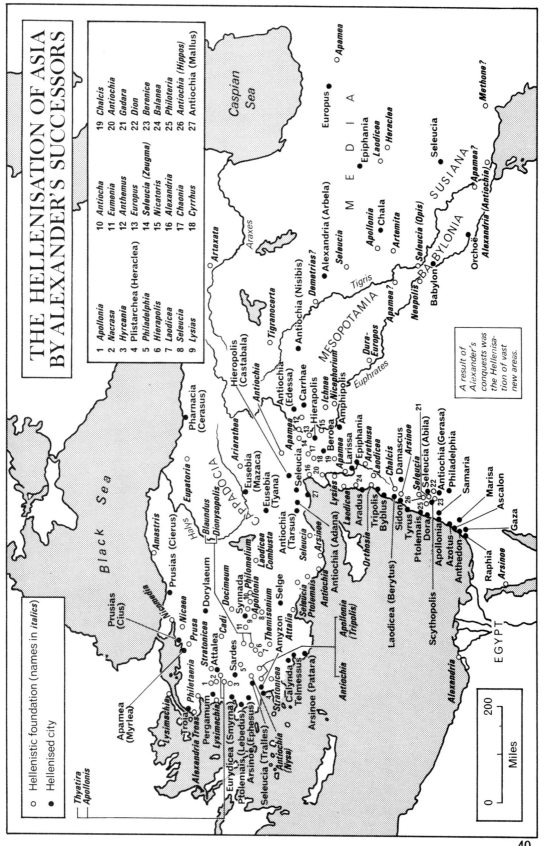

THE HELLENISATION OF ASIA BY ALEXANDER'S SUCCESSORS

1 Apollonia
2 Nacrasa
3 Hyrcania
4 Plistarchea (Heraclea)
5 Philadelphia
6 Hierapolis
7 Laodicea
8 Seleucia
9 Lysias

10 Antiocha
11 Eumenia
12 Anthemus
13 Europus
14 Seleucia (Zeugma)
15 Nicatoris
16 Alexandria
17 Chaonia
18 Cyrrhus

19 Chalcis
20 Antiochia
21 Gadara
22 Dion
23 Berenice
24 Balanea
25 Philoteria
26 Antiochia (Hippos)
27 Antiochia (Mallus)

○ Hellenistic foundation (names in *italics*)
● Hellenised city

Thyatira
Apollonis

A result of Alexander's conquests was the Hellenisation of vast new areas.

0 ___ 200
Miles

40

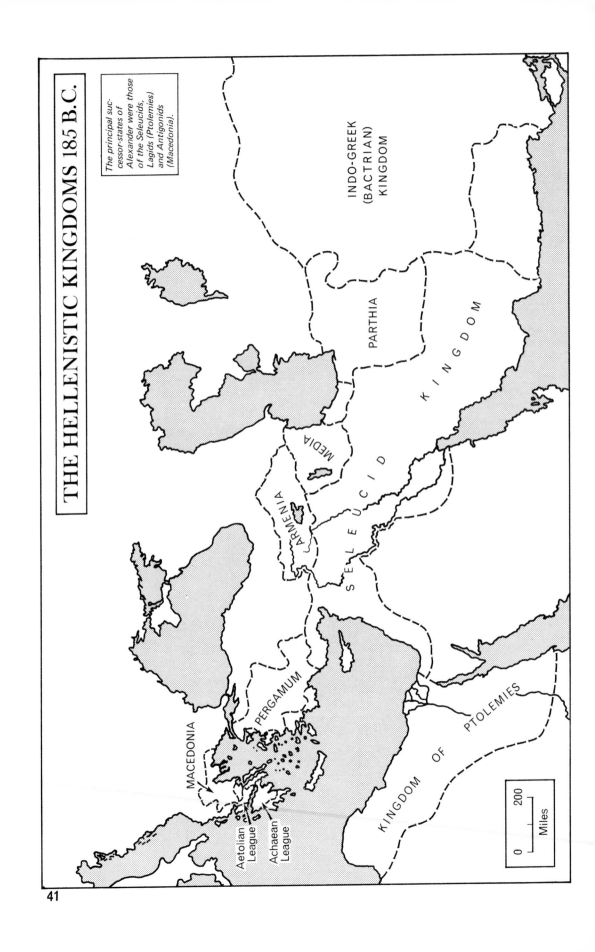

THE HELLENISTIC KINGDOMS 185 B.C.

The principal successor-states of Alexander were those of the Seleucids, Lagids (Ptolemies) and Antigonids (Macedonia).

INDO-GREEK (BACTRIAN) KINGDOM

PARTHIA

SELEUCID KINGDOM

MEDIA

ARMENIA

MACEDONIA

PERGAMUM

Aetolian League

Achaean League

KINGDOM OF PTOLEMIES

0   200

Miles

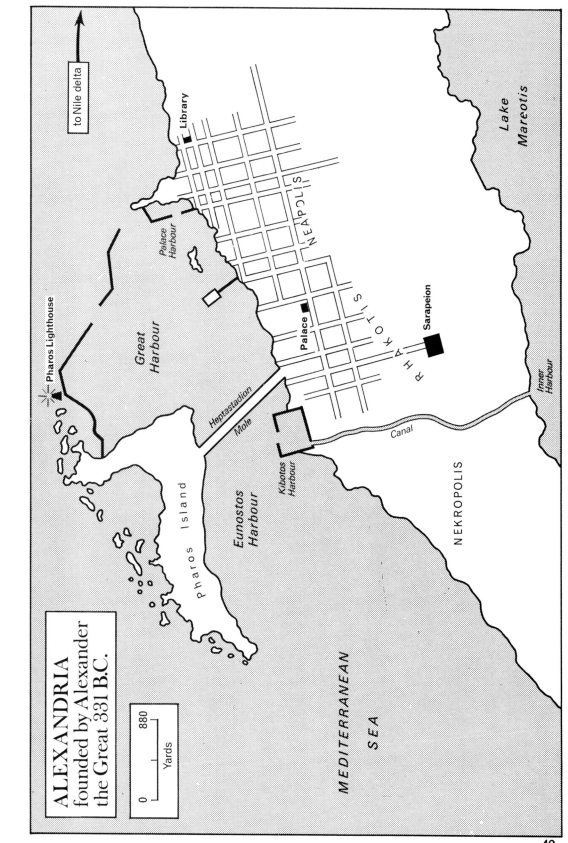

ALEXANDRIA
founded by Alexander
the Great 331 B.C.

0   880
Yards

to Nile delta

Pharos Lighthouse

Library

Palace

Palace Harbour

Great Harbour

Heptastadion

Male

Pharos Island

Eunostos Harbour

Kibotos Harbour

NEAPOLIS

RHAKOTIS

Sarapeion

Canal

Inner Harbour

NEKROPOLIS

Lake Mareotis

MEDITERRANEAN SEA

42

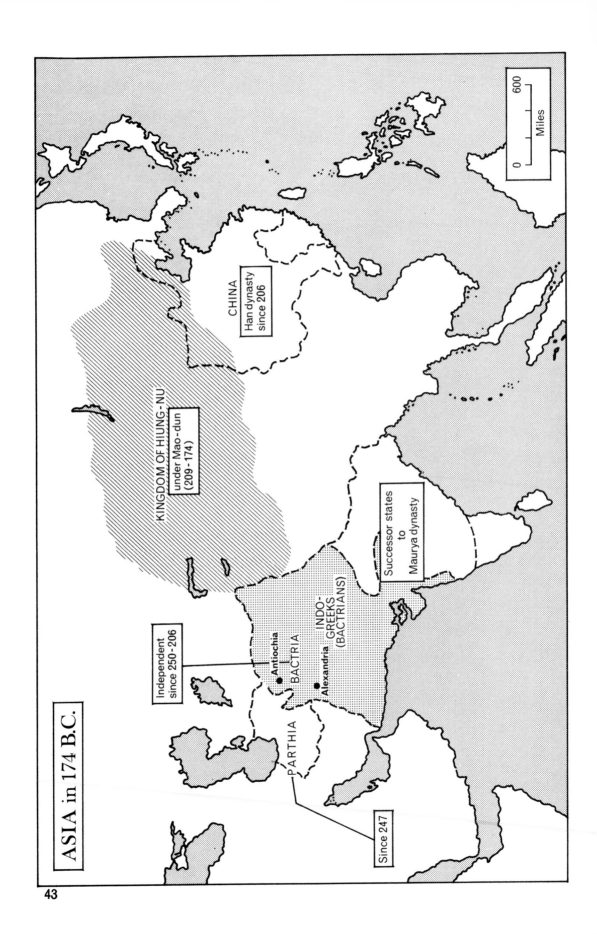

ASIA in 174 B.C.

KINGDOM OF HIUNG-NU
under Mao-dun
(209-174)

CHINA
Han dynasty
since 206

Successor states
to
Maurya dynasty

INDO-
GREEKS
(BACTRIANS)

Independent
since 250-206

Antiochia

BACTRIA

Alexandria

PARTHIA

Since 247

600

0

Miles

43

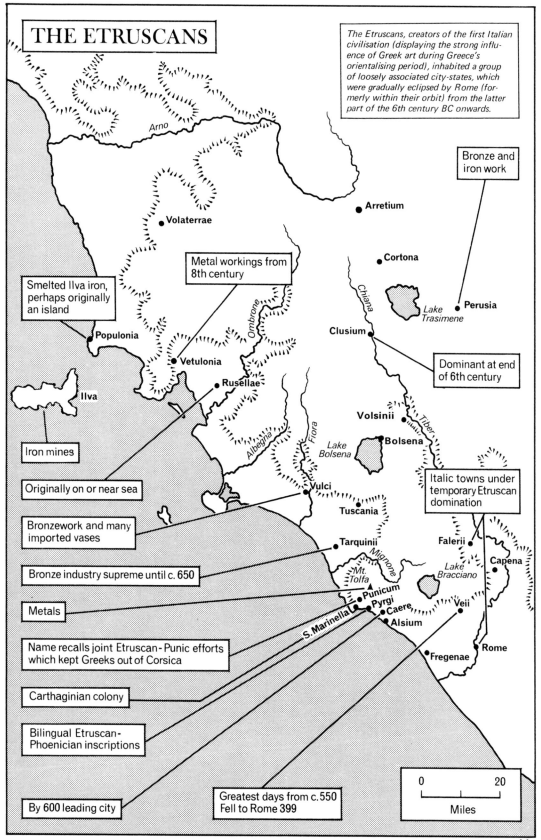

THE ETRUSCANS

The Etruscans, creators of the first Italian civilisation (displaying the strong influence of Greek art during Greece's orientalising period), inhabited a group of loosely associated city-states, which were gradually eclipsed by Rome (formerly within their orbit) from the latter part of the 6th century BC onwards.

Arno

Bronze and iron work

Volaterrae

Arretium

Cortona

Metal workings from 8th century

Chiana

Lake Trasimene

Perusia

Smelted Ilva iron, perhaps originally an island

Ombrone

Clusium

Dominant at end of 6th century

Populonia

Vetulonia

Rusellae

Volsinii

Tiber

Ilva

Bolsena

Lake Bolsena

Iron mines

Albegna

Fiora

Italic towns under temporary Etruscan domination

Originally on or near sea

Vulci

Tuscania

Falerii

Lake Bracciano

Capena

Bronzework and many imported vases

Tarquinii

Mignone

Bronze industry supreme until c.650

Mt. Tolfa

Punicum

Veii

Metals

Pyrgi

Caere

S.Marinella

Alsium

Rome

Name recalls joint Etruscan-Punic efforts which kept Greeks out of Corsica

Fregenae

Carthaginian colony

Bilingual Etruscan-Phoenician inscriptions

By 600 leading city

Greatest days from c.550 Fell to Rome 399

0   20
Miles

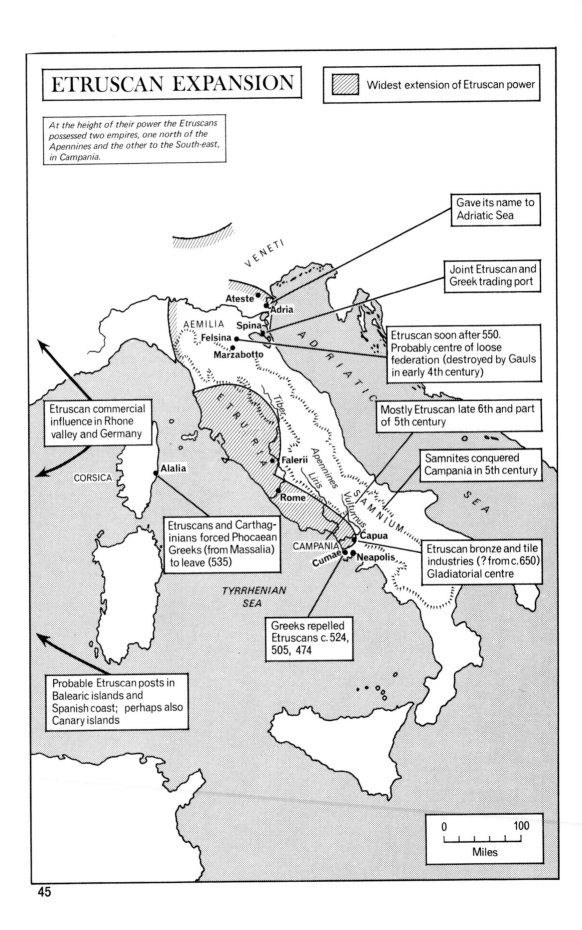

ETRUSCAN EXPANSION

Widest extension of Etruscan power

At the height of their power the Etruscans possessed two empires, one north of the Apennines and the other to the South-east, in Campania.

VENETI

Ateste

Adria
Gave its name to Adriatic Sea

AEMILIA

Spina
Joint Etruscan and Greek trading port

Felsina

Marzabotto
Etruscan soon after 550. Probably centre of loose federation (destroyed by Gauls in early 4th century)

ADRIATIC

Etruscan commercial influence in Rhone valley and Germany

Tiber

ETRURIA

Mostly Etruscan late 6th and part of 5th century

Samnites conquered Campania in 5th century

CORSICA

Alalia

Falerii

Apennines

Liris

Rome

Vulturnus

SAMNIUM

SEA

Etruscans and Carthaginians forced Phocaean Greeks (from Massalia) to leave (535)

CAMPANIA

Capua

Cumae

Neapolis

Etruscan bronze and tile industries (? from c. 650) Gladiatorial centre

TYRRHENIAN SEA

Greeks repelled Etruscans c. 524, 505, 474

Probable Etruscan posts in Balearic islands and Spanish coast; perhaps also Canary islands

0   100
Miles

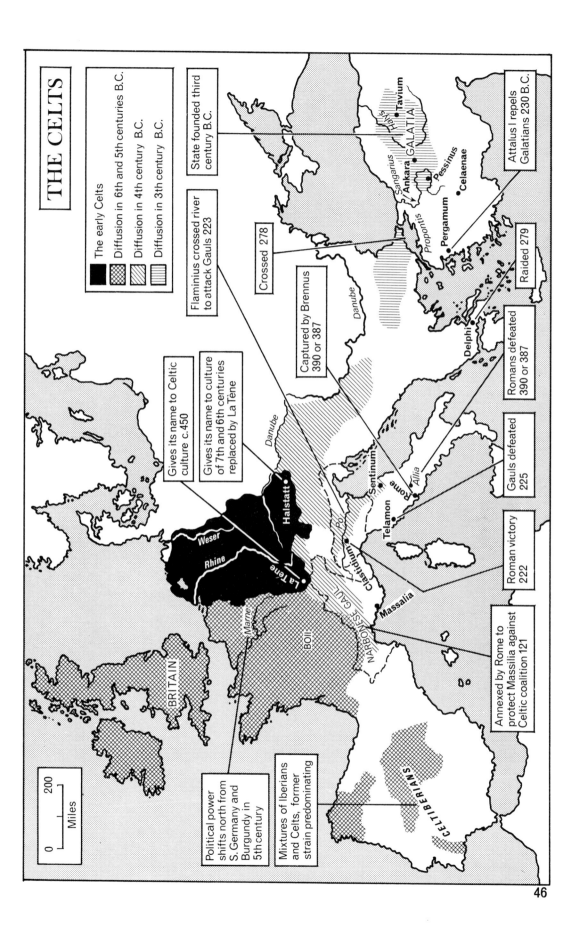

THE CELTS

The early Celts

Diffusion in 6th and 5th centuries B.C.

Diffusion in 4th century B.C.

Diffusion in 3th century B.C.

State founded third century B.C.

Flaminius crossed river to attack Gauls 223

Crossed 278

Captured by Brennus 390 or 387

Gives its name to Celtic culture c.450

Gives its name to culture of 7th and 6th centuries replaced by La Tène

Political power shifts north from S. Germany and Burgundy in 5th century

Mixtures of Iberians and Celts, former strain predominating

Annexed by Rome to protect Massilia against Celtic coalition 121

Roman victory 222

Gauls defeated 225

Romans defeated 390 or 387

Raided 279

Attalus I repels Galatians 230 B.C.

GALATIA

Tavium

Ankara

Pessinus

Celaenae

Pergamum

Propontis

Halys

Sangarius

Danube

Delphi

Sentinum

Rome

Allia

Telamon

Clastidium

Cisalpine GAUL

Po

Massilia

NARBONESE GAUL

Boii

Marne

Rhine

Weser

Halstatt

La Tène

Danube

BRITAIN

CELTIBERIANS

Miles

0   200

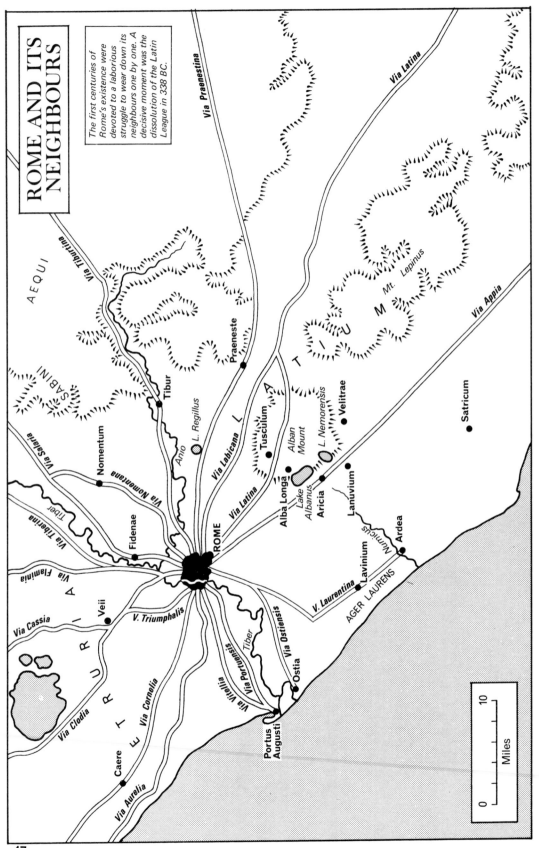

ROME AND ITS NEIGHBOURS

The first centuries of Rome's existence were devoted to a laborious struggle to wear down its neighbours one by one. A decisive moment was the dissolution of the Latin League in 338 BC.

AEQUI

SABINI

Via Tiburtina

Via Praenestina

Via Latina

Tibur

L. Regillus

Praeneste

Anio

Via Salaria

Nomentum

Via Nomentana

L A T I U M

Tusculum

Mt. Lepinus

Fidenae

Via Labicana

Alban Mount

L. Nemorensis

Velitrae

Via Tiberina

Tiber

Via Latina

Alba Longa

Lake Albanus

Aricia

Lanuvium

Satricum

Via Flaminia

ROME

Via Appia

E T R U R I A

Veii

V. Triumphalis

Numicus

Ardea

Via Cassia

Via Vitellia

Via Portuensis

Via Ostiensis

V. Laurentina

Lavinium

Via Clodia

Via Cornelia

Tiber

AGER LAURENS

Caere

Ostia

Portus Augusti

Via Aurelia

0   10
|——————————|
Miles

47

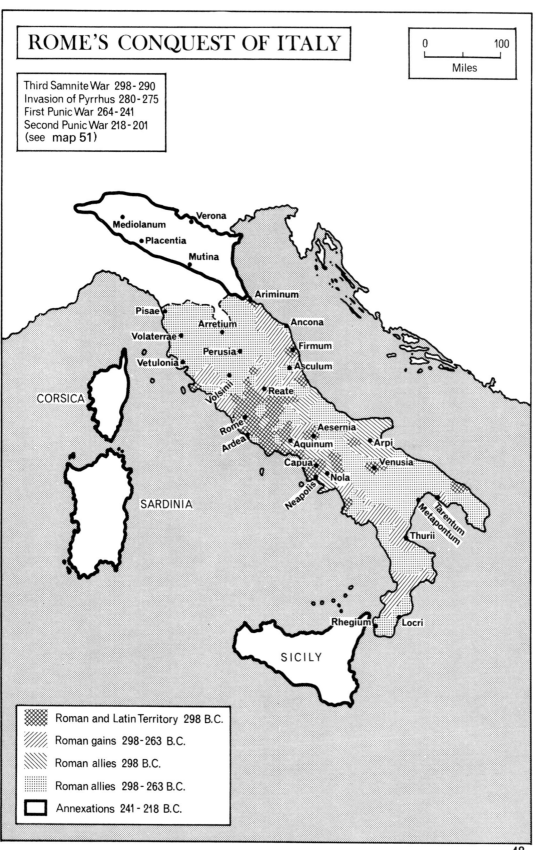

ROME'S CONQUEST OF ITALY

Third Samnite War 298-290
Invasion of Pyrrhus 280-275
First Punic War 264-241
Second Punic War 218-201
(see **map 51**)

0   100
Miles

Verona
Mediolanum
Placentia
Mutina
Ariminum
Pisae
Arretium
Ancona
Volaterrae
Perusia
Firmum
Vetulonia
Asculum
Volsinii
Reate
CORSICA
Rome
Aesernia
Ardea
Aquinum
Arpi
Venusia
Capua
SARDINIA
Nola
Neapolis
Tarentum
Metapontum
Thurii
Rhegium
Locri
SICILY

Roman and Latin Territory 298 B.C.
Roman gains 298-263 B.C.
Roman allies 298 B.C.
Roman allies 298-263 B.C.
Annexations 241-218 B.C.

48

THE ROADS OF ROMAN ITALY

0   100
Miles

Augusta Praetoria
Mediolanum
Segusio
Verona
(6)
(1)
Aquileia
Dertona
Placentia
Cremona
(6)
Mantua
Genua
Po
(1)
Ravenna
(8)
Luna
Florentia
Ariminum
Pisae
Fanum Fortunae
Vada Volaterrana
Arretium
(11)
(4)
Truentum
(3)
Reate
(13)
Aternum
Tibur
(7)
Corfinium
ROME
Anagnia
(5)
Fregellae
(2)
Canusium
Tarracina
Cales
Capua
Beneventum
(10)
Casilinum
Neapolis
Venusia
(2)
Brundisium
(12)
Tarentum
(9)
Rhegium

CORSICA

SARDINIA

ADRIATIC SEA

TYRRHENIAN SEA

SICILY

(1) Via Aemilia (187 B.C.) **(8)** Via Julia Augusta
(2) Via Appia (312 - 244 B.C.) **(9)** Via Domitiana
(3) Via Aurelia **(10)** Via Trajana
(4) Via Flaminia (220 B.C.) **(11)** Via Cassia
(5) Via Latina **(12)** Via Popillia
(6) Via Postumia (148 B.C.) **(13)** Via Salaria
(7) Via Valeria

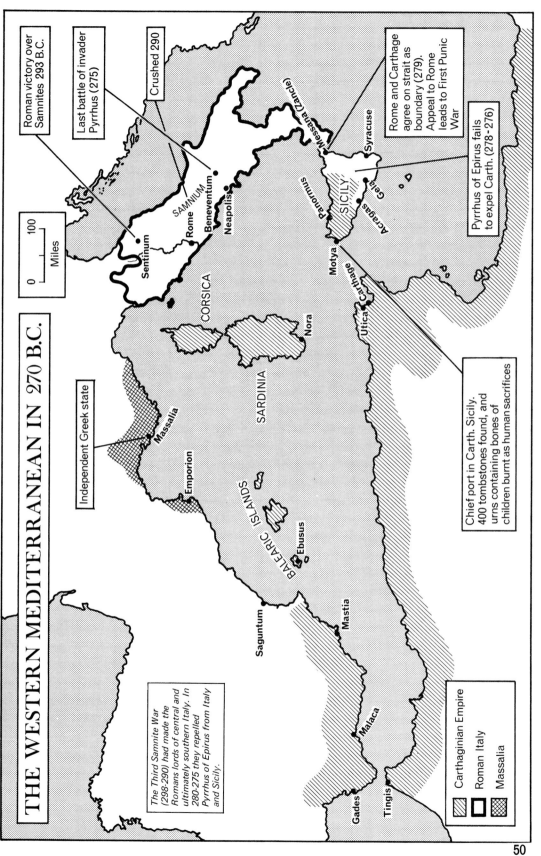

THE WESTERN MEDITERRANEAN IN 270 B.C.

Roman victory over Samnites 293 B.C.

Last battle of invader Pyrrhus (275)

Crushed 290

Rome and Carthage agree on strait as boundary (279). Appeal to Rome leads to First Punic War

Pyrrhus of Epirus fails to expel Carth. (278 - 276)

SAMNIUM

Beneventum

Rome

Neapolis

Sentinum

Messana (Zancle)

Syracuse

Gela

SICILY

Acragas

Panormus

Motya

Utica Carthage

CORSICA

Independent Greek state

Massalia

Emporion

SARDINIA

Nora

Chief port in Carth. Sicily, 400 tombstones found, and urns containing bones of children burnt as human sacrifices

BALEARIC ISLANDS

Ebusus

Saguntum

Mastia

The Third Samnite War (298-290) had made the Romans lords of central and ultimately southern Italy. In 280-275 they repelled Pyrrhus of Epirus from Italy and Sicily.

Malaca

Gades

Tingis

		Carthaginian Empire
		Roman Italy
		Massalia

0   100

Miles

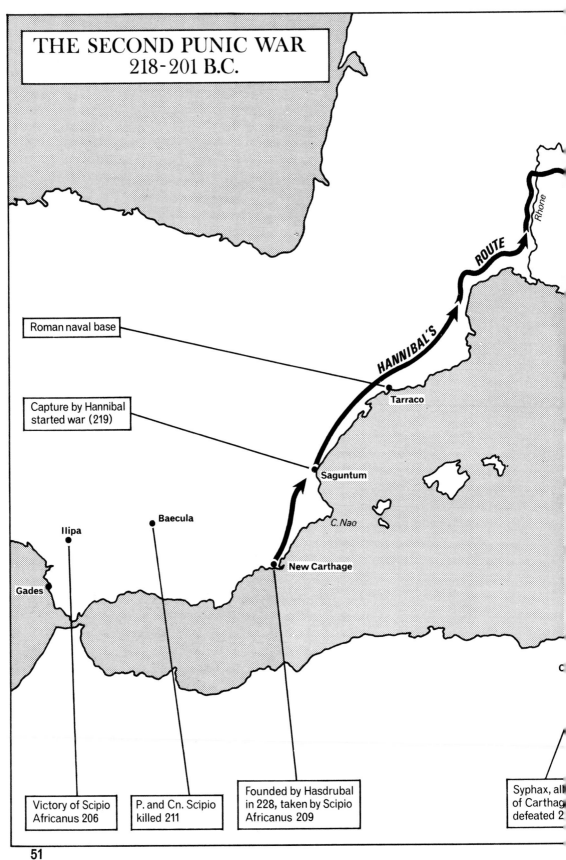

THE SECOND PUNIC WAR
218-201 B.C.

HANNIBAL'S ROUTE

Rhone

Roman naval base

Tarraco

Capture by Hannibal started war (219)

Saguntum

C. Nao

Baecula

Ilipa

Gades

New Carthage

Victory of Scipio Africanus 206

P. and Cn. Scipio killed 211

Founded by Hasdrubal in 228, taken by Scipio Africanus 209

Syphax, all of Carthag defeated 2

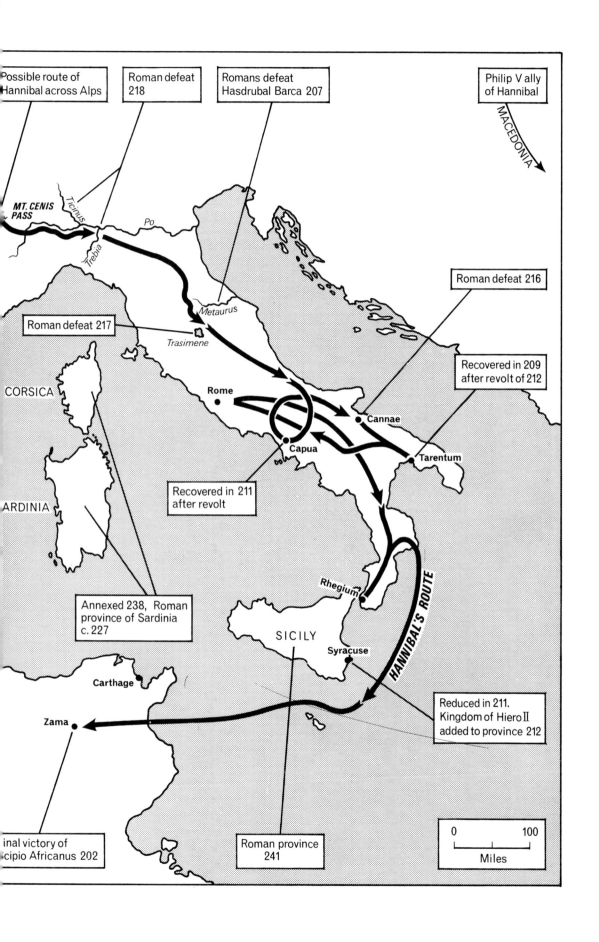

Possible route of
Hannibal across Alps

Roman defeat
218

Romans defeat
Hasdrubal Barca 207

Philip V ally
of Hannibal

MACEDONIA

MT. CENIS
PASS

Ticinus

Po

Trebia

Metaurus

Roman defeat 217

Trasimene

Roman defeat 216

CORSICA

Rome

Recovered in 209
after revolt of 212

Cannae

ARDINIA

Capua

Tarentum

Recovered in 211
after revolt

Annexed 238, Roman
province of Sardinia
c. 227

Rhegium

HANNIBAL'S ROUTE

SICILY

Syracuse

Reduced in 211.
Kingdom of Hiero II
added to province 212

Carthage

Zama

inal victory of
cipio Africanus 202

Roman province
241

0   100

Miles

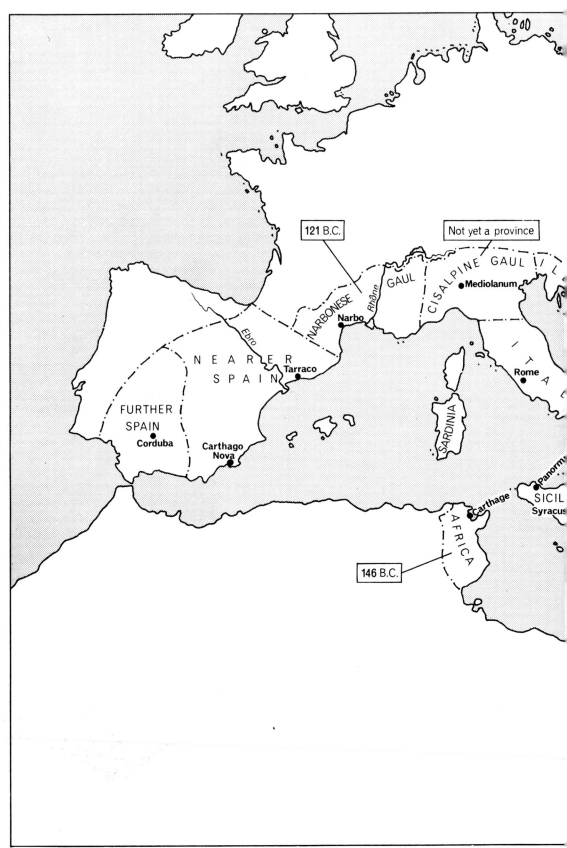

121 B.C.

Not yet a province

GAUL

NARBONESE
Rhône

CISALPINE GAUL

Mediolanum

Narbo

Ebro

N E A R E R
S P A I N

Tarraco

Rome

FURTHER
SPAIN

Corduba

Carthago
Nova

SARDINIA

Panorm

SICIL

Carthage

Syracus

AFRICA

146 B.C.

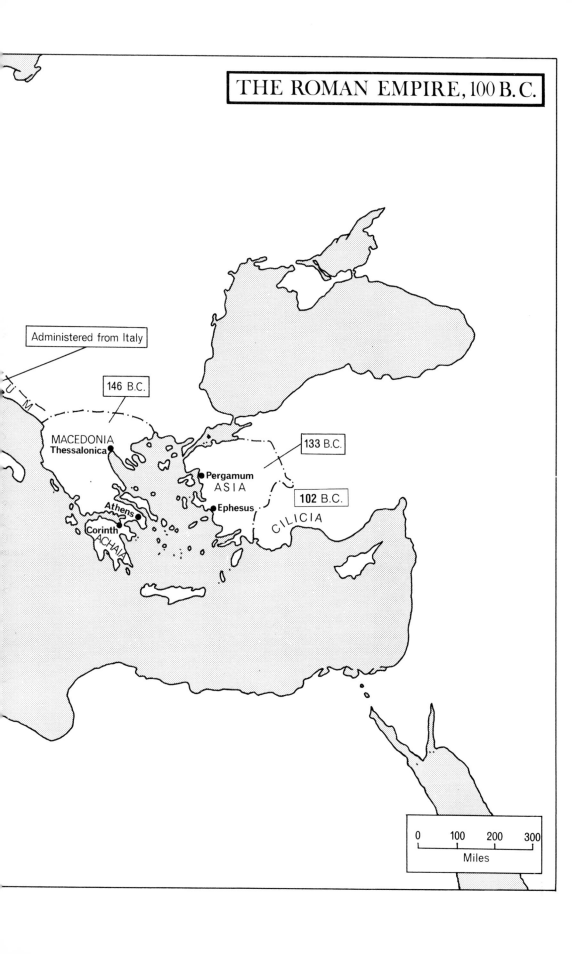

THE ROMAN EMPIRE, 100 B.C.

Administered from Italy

146 B.C.

133 B.C.

102 B.C.

MACEDONIA
Thessalonica

Pergamum
ASIA

Ephesus

CILICIA

Athens

Corinth
ACHAIA

0   100   200   300

Miles

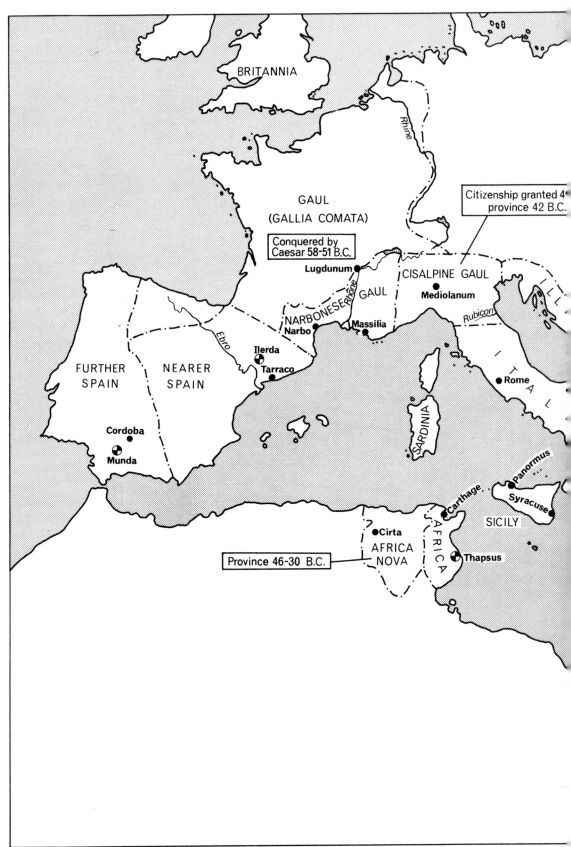

BRITANNIA

GAUL
(GALLIA COMATA)

Conquered by
Caesar 58-51 B.C.

Citizenship granted 4*
province 42 B.C.

Lugdunum

CISALPINE GAUL

Mediolanum

NARBONESE GAUL

Rubicon

Narbo

Massilia

Ilerda

Tarraco

Rome

FURTHER
SPAIN

NEARER
SPAIN

Ebro

Rhine

Rhône

SARDINIA

ITALY

Cordoba

Munda

Panormus

Carthage

Syracuse

Cirta

AFRICA
NOVA

AFRICA

SICILY

Thapsus

Province 46-30 B.C.

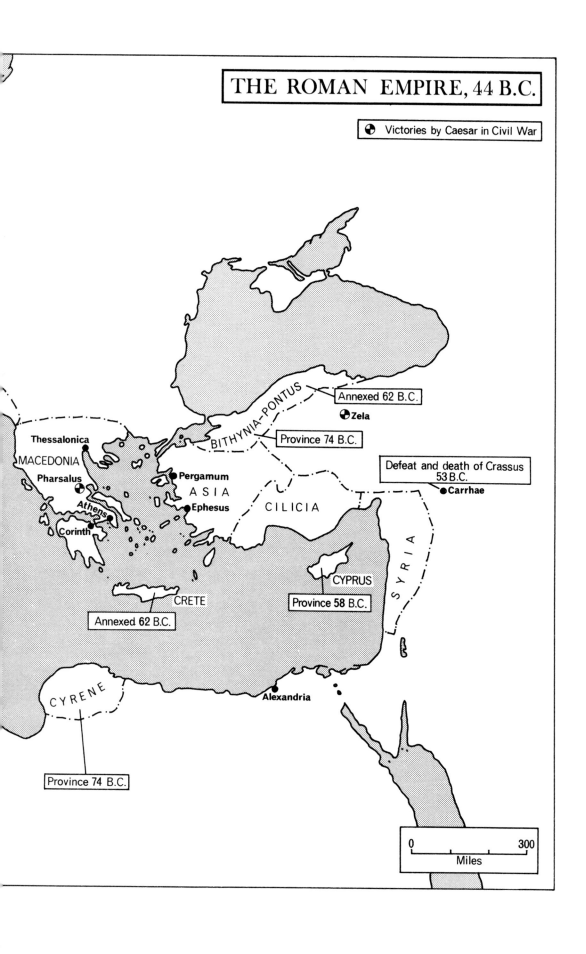

THE ROMAN EMPIRE, 44 B.C.

◐ Victories by Caesar in Civil War

BITHYNIA-PONTUS

Annexed 62 B.C.

◐ Zela

Province 74 B.C.

Defeat and death of Crassus
53 B.C.
● Carrhae

Thessalonica
MACEDONIA
Pharsalus
Pergamum
ASIA
Athens
● Ephesus
Corinth
CILICIA

SYRIA

CYPRUS
Province 58 B.C.

CRETE
Annexed 62 B.C.

CYRENE

Alexandria

Province 74 B.C.

0   300
Miles

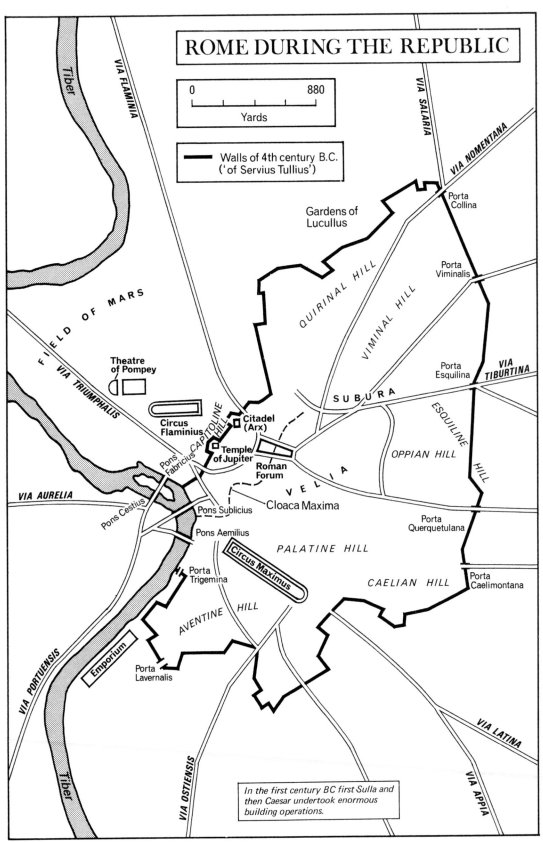

ROME DURING THE REPUBLIC

0 ——————— 880
Yards

Walls of 4th century B.C.
('of Servius Tullius')

Tiber

VIA FLAMINIA

VIA SALARIA

VIA NOMENTANA

Porta
Collina

Gardens of
Lucullus

QUIRINAL HILL

VIMINAL HILL

Porta
Viminalis

FIELD OF MARS

VIA TRIUMPHALIS

Theatre
of Pompey

Circus
Flaminius

CAPITOLINE HILL

Citadel
(Arx)

Temple
of Jupiter

Roman
Forum

SUBURA

Porta
Esquilina

VIA
TIBURTINA

ESQUILINE HILL

OPPIAN HILL

VELIA

Pons
Fabricius

VIA AURELIA

Pons Cestius

Pons Sublicius

Pons Aemilius

Cloaca Maxima

Porta
Querquetulana

PALATINE HILL

Circus Maximus

CAELIAN HILL

Porta
Caelimontana

Porta
Trigemina

AVENTINE HILL

Emporium

Porta
Lavernalis

VIA PORTUENSIS

VIA OSTIENSIS

Tiber

VIA LATINA

VIA APPIA

In the first century BC first Sulla and
then Caesar undertook enormous
building operations.

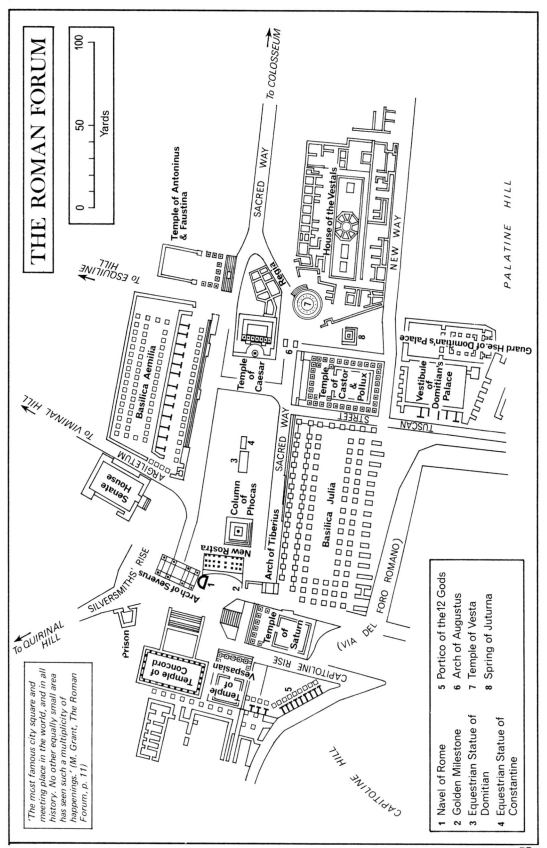

THE ROMAN FORUM

Yards
0 50 100

'The most famous city square and meeting place in the world, and in all history. No other equally small area has seen such a multiplicity of happenings.' (M. Grant, The Roman Forum, p. 11)

To ESQUILINE HILL

To VIMINAL HILL

To QUIRINAL HILL

Temple of Antoninus & Faustina

Basilica Aemilia

ARGILETUM

Senate House

SILVERSMITHS' RISE

Arch of Severus

Prison

Temple of Concord

Temple of Vespasian

CAPITOLINE RISE

CAPITOLINE HILL

Temple of Saturn

Arch of Tiberius

New Rostra

Column of Phocas

Temple of Caesar

Regia

SACRED WAY

Basilica Julia

STREET

TUSCAN

(VIA DEL FORO ROMANO)

Temple of Castor & Pollux

House of the Vestals

SACRED WAY

To COLOSSEUM

NEW WAY

Vestibule of Domitian's Palace

Guard Hse. of Domitian's Palace

PALATINE HILL

3 4
5 6 7 8

1 Navel of Rome
2 Golden Milestone
3 Equestrian Statue of Domitian
4 Equestrian Statue of Constantine
5 Portico of the 12 Gods
6 Arch of Augustus
7 Temple of Vesta
8 Spring of Juturna

55

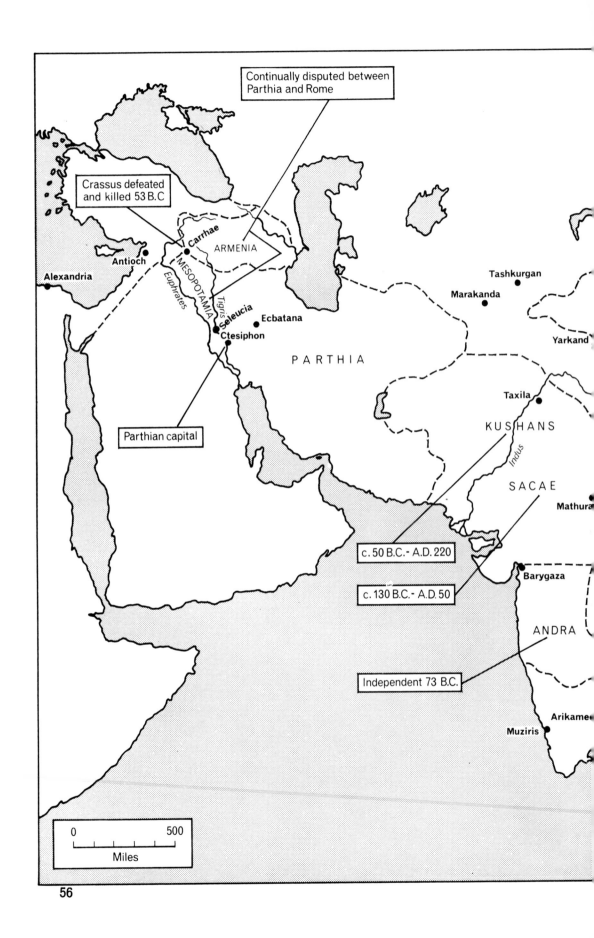

Continually disputed between
Parthia and Rome

Crassus defeated
and killed 53 B.C

Alexandria

Antioch

Carrhae

ARMENIA

MESOPOTAMIA

Euphrates

Tigris

Seleucia

Ecbatana

Ctesiphon

Parthian capital

PARTHIA

Tashkurgan

Marakanda

Yarkand

Taxila

KUSHANS

Indus

SACAE

Mathura

c. 50 B.C.- A.D. 220

c. 130 B.C.- A.D. 50

Barygaza

ANDRA

Independent 73 B.C.

Arikame

Muziris

0   500
Miles

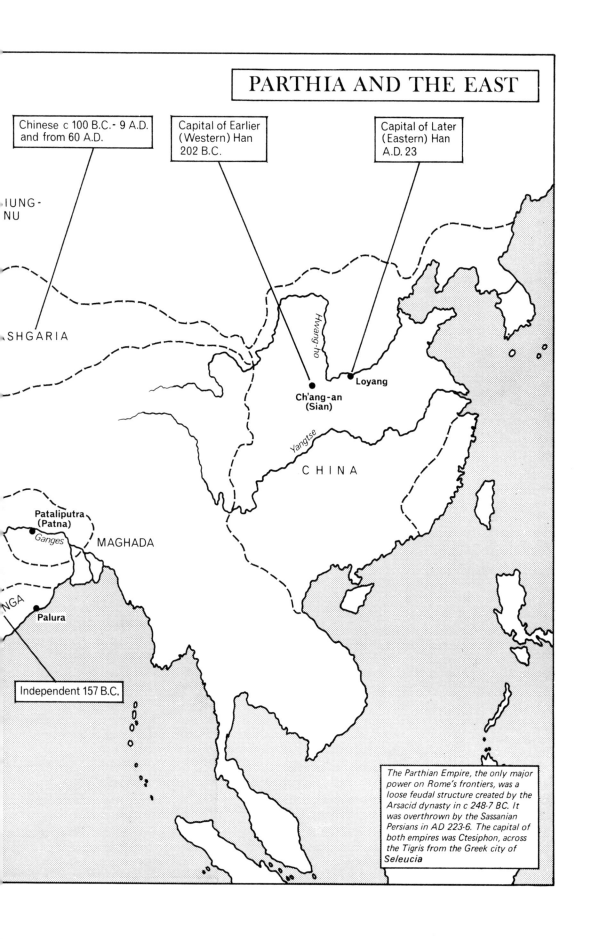

PARTHIA AND THE EAST

Chinese c 100 B.C.- 9 A.D. and from 60 A.D.

Capital of Earlier (Western) Han 202 B.C.

Capital of Later (Eastern) Han A.D. 23

IUNG-NU

SHGARIA

Hwang-ho

Loyang

Ch'ang-an (Sian)

Yangtse

C H I N A

Pataliputra (Patna)

Ganges

MAGHADA

NGA

Palura

Independent 157 B.C.

The Parthian Empire, the only major power on Rome's frontiers, was a loose feudal structure created by the Arsacid dynasty in c 248-7 BC. It was overthrown by the Sassanian Persians in AD 223-6. The capital of both empires was Ctesiphon, across the Tigris from the Greek city of Seleucia

BRITANNIA

LWR.
GERMANY
(17 B.C.)

FREE
GERMANY

Temporarily conquered from
15 B.C. but abandoned after
ambushing of Varus by
Arminius in A.D.9

Colonia
Agrippinensis

Rhine

B E L G I C A

Moguntiacum

LOWER
PANNONIA
(10
B.C.

LUGDUNENSIS

Danube

UPR.
GERMANY
(17 B.C.)

RHAETIA
(15 B.C.)

NORICUM
(15 B.C.)

UPPER
PANNONIA

P

Aquileia

Lugdunum

AQUITANIA

C

M

Adriatic
Sea

NARBONENSIS

Nemausus

I
T
A
L
Y

Rome

T A R R A C O N E N S I S

Tarraco

LUSITANIA
(c. 27 B.C.)

Naulochus

SICILY

Corduba

BAETICA

Carthage

Gades

Naval victory ove
Sextus Pompeiu
36 B.C.

M A U R E T A N I A

A
F
R
I
C
A

——————— Imperial frontier as in A.D. 14

– – – – Provincial frontiers

ASIA Senatorial provinces

ALPINE PROVINCES (15-14 B.C.)
M: Maritime, C: Cottian, P: Pennine

*The hatched areas represent the
more important dependent ('client')
states, whose monarchs enjoyed
internal autonomy but had to
support Rome's foreign policy and
help defend the imperial frontiers.*

///// Principal client states

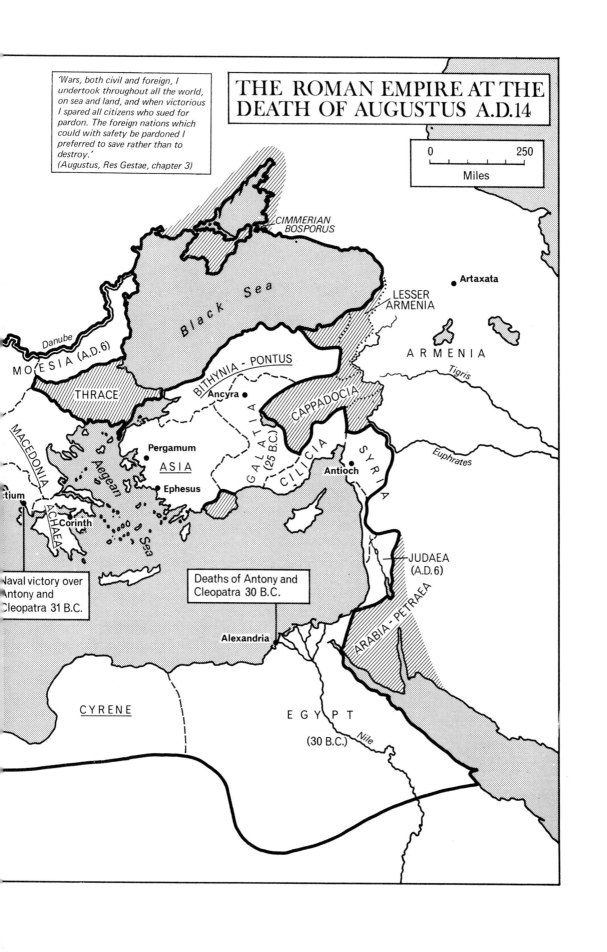

THE ROMAN EMPIRE AT THE DEATH OF AUGUSTUS A.D.14

'Wars, both civil and foreign, I undertook throughout all the world, on sea and land, and when victorious I spared all citizens who sued for pardon. The foreign nations which could with safety be pardoned I preferred to save rather than to destroy.'
(Augustus, Res Gestae, chapter 3)

0   250
Miles

CIMMERIAN BOSPORUS

Black Sea

• Artaxata

LESSER ARMENIA

A R M E N I A

Danube

MOESIA (A.D.6)

Tigris

THRACE

BITHYNIA - PONTUS

Ancyra •

CAPPADOCIA

MACEDONIA

GALATIA (25 B.C.)

CILICIA

S Y R I A

Euphrates

Pergamum •

A S I A

Antioch •

Aegean Sea

• Ephesus

tium

ACHAEA

• Corinth

JUDAEA (A.D.6)

Naval victory over Antony and Cleopatra 31 B.C.

Deaths of Antony and Cleopatra 30 B.C.

ARABIA - PETRAEA

Alexandria

CYRENE

E G Y P T

(30 B.C.)

Nile

GAUL

Rhine

Danube

Arelate *VIA DOMITIA*

Narbo

Forum
Julii

Rhone

Ebro

SPAIN

Rome

Adriatic
Sea

ITALY

Tyrrhenian
Sea

M e d i t e r r a n e a n

AFRICA

⎯⎯⎯ Imperial frontier as in A.D. 14

══ Roman roads

ⁿⁿⁿⁿ Mountain contours

*All roads lead to Rome: the most
potent guarantees of external and
internal peace and stimulants of
prosperity.*

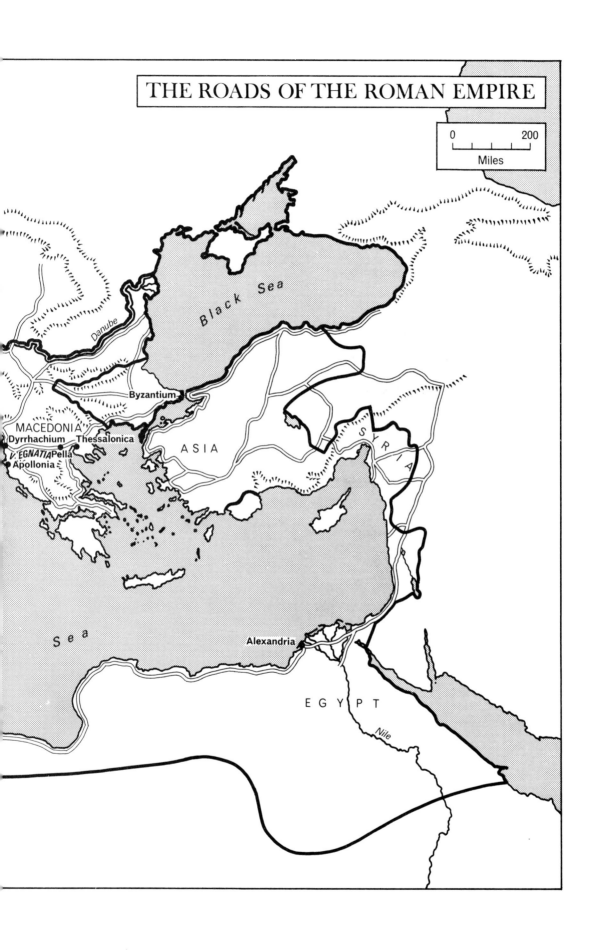

THE ROADS OF THE ROMAN EMPIRE

0   200
Miles

Danube

Black Sea

Byzantium

MACEDONIA
Dyrrhachium   Thessalonica
*V. EGNATIA*Pella
Apollonia

ASIA

S Y R I A

Sea

Alexandria

E G Y P T

Nile

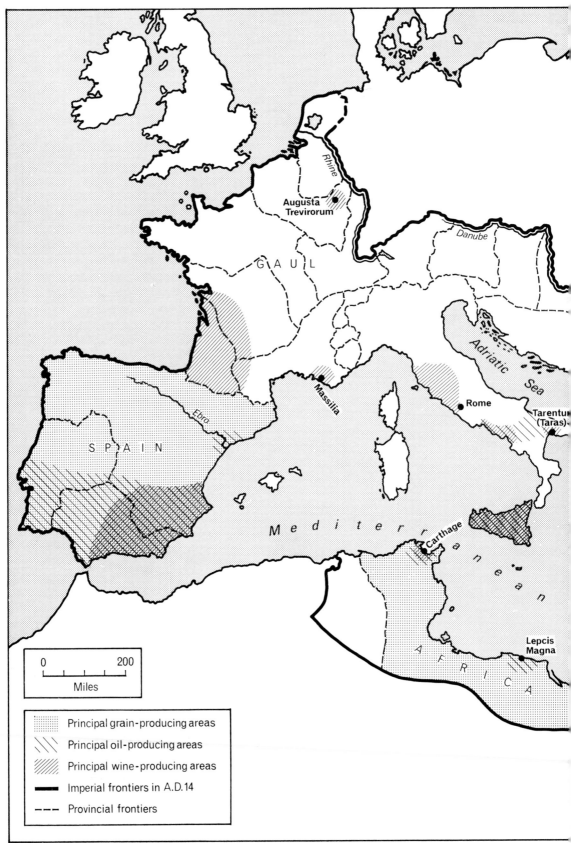

Rhine

Augusta
Trevirorum

Danube

GAUL

Adriatic Sea

Massilia

Rome

Tarentu
(Taras)

Ebro

SPAIN

Mediterranean

Carthage

Lepcis
Magna

AFRICA

0   200
       Miles

Principal grain-producing areas

Principal oil-producing areas

Principal wine-producing areas

Imperial frontiers in A.D.14

Provincial frontiers

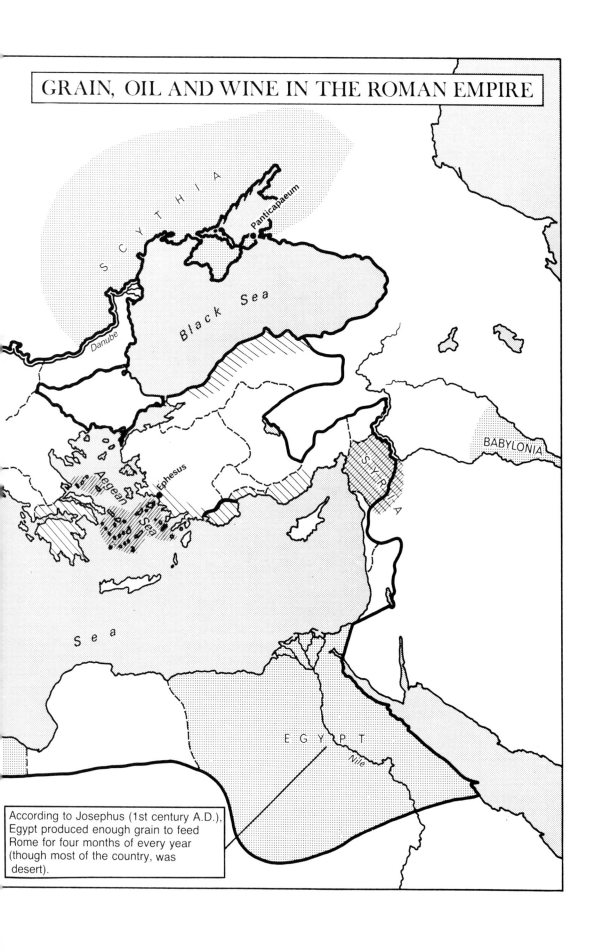

GRAIN, OIL AND WINE IN THE ROMAN EMPIRE

S C Y T H I A

Panticapaeum

Black Sea

Danube

BABYLONIA

S Y R I A

Aegean Sea

Ephesus

Sea

Sea

E G Y P T

Nile

According to Josephus (1st century A.D.),
Egypt produced enough grain to feed
Rome for four months of every year
(though most of the country, was
desert).

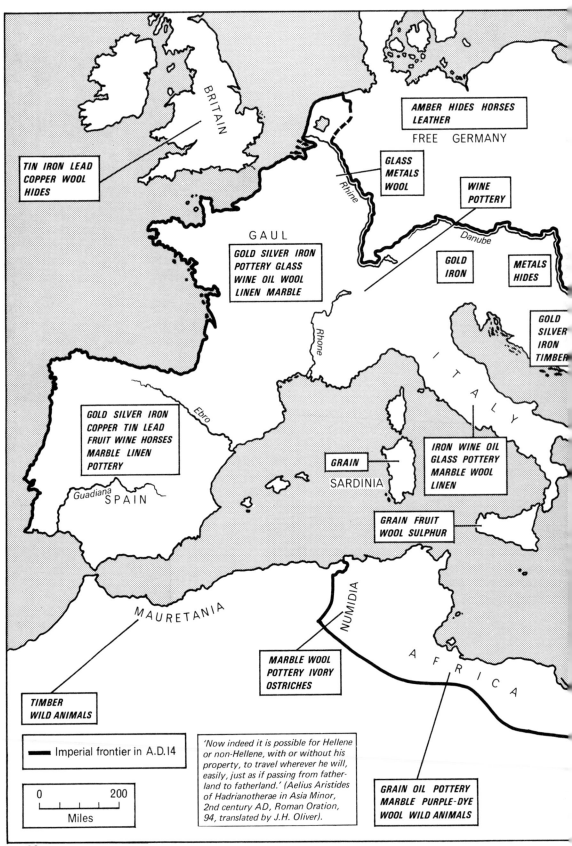

BRITAIN

TIN IRON LEAD
COPPER WOOL
HIDES

AMBER HIDES HORSES
LEATHER

FREE GERMANY

GLASS
METALS
WOOL

Rhine

WINE
POTTERY

GAUL

GOLD SILVER IRON
POTTERY GLASS
WINE OIL WOOL
LINEN MARBLE

Danube

GOLD
IRON

METALS
HIDES

GOLD
SILVER
IRON
TIMBER

Rhone

ITALY

GOLD SILVER IRON
COPPER TIN LEAD
FRUIT WINE HORSES
MARBLE LINEN
POTTERY

Ebro

GRAIN

SARDINIA

IRON WINE OIL
GLASS POTTERY
MARBLE WOOL
LINEN

Guadiana SPAIN

GRAIN FRUIT
WOOL SULPHUR

MAURETANIA

NUMIDIA

AFRICA

MARBLE WOOL
POTTERY IVORY
OSTRICHES

TIMBER
WILD ANIMALS

━━━ Imperial frontier in A.D. 14

'Now indeed it is possible for Hellene
or non-Hellene, with or without his
property, to travel wherever he will,
easily, just as if passing from fatherland to fatherland.' (Aelius Aristides
of Hadrianotherae in Asia Minor,
2nd century AD, Roman Oration,
94, translated by J.H. Oliver).

0   200

Miles

GRAIN OIL POTTERY
MARBLE PURPLE-DYE
WOOL WILD ANIMALS

TRADING PRODUCTS IN THE ROMAN EMPIRE

Dnieper

Bug

GOLD TIMBER
HORSES SALT

Dniester

S C Y T H I A

**GRAIN HONEY HEMP
NUTS HIDES**

IRON

CAUCASUS

SILK
from China

D A C I A

GRAIN FISH GOLD
SILVER IRON LEAD

ARMENIA — IRON

Danube

Black Sea

METALS BITUMEN
PRECIOUS STONES

OESIA

THRACE

GRAIN FISH
HORSES

MESOPOTAMIA

Tigris

S
Y
R
I
A

ASIA

MACEDONIA

WOOL LINEN WINE
OIL MARBLE POTTERY
PARCHMENT TIMBER
HORSES EMERALDS
GOLD SILVER IRON

Euphrates

SILK from China

GREECE

CYPRUS

WINE HONEY LINEN
PURPLE-DYE
POTTERY
MARBLE

COPPER OIL

JUDAEA

WOOL PURPLE-DYE
LINEN GLASS
POTTERY TIMBER
LEATHER-GOODS

ARABIA

ASPHALT

FRANKINCENSE AND
OTHER PERFUMES

CYRENE

EGYPT

GLASS GRAIN LINEN
TEXTILES DRUGS PAPYRUS
WILD ANIMALS PORPHYRY

PEPPER from India

*to South
Arabia*

SILPHIUM [Medicinal
herb] TIMBER

*IVORY from
Central Africa*

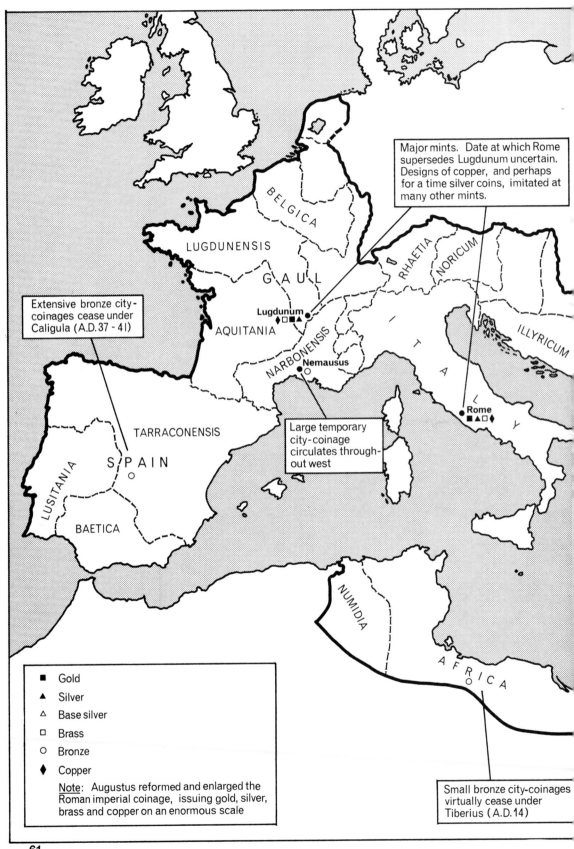

Major mints. Date at which Rome supersedes Lugdunum uncertain. Designs of copper, and perhaps for a time silver coins, imitated at many other mints.

BELGICA

LUGDUNENSIS

G A U L

RHAETIA

NORICUM

I T A L Y

ILLYRICUM

Extensive bronze city-coinages cease under Caligula (A.D. 37-41)

Lugdunum
♦ □ ■ ▲

AQUITANIA

NARBONENSIS

Nemausus
○

Rome
■ ▲ □ ♦

Large temporary city-coinage circulates through-out west

TARRACONENSIS

S P A I N
○

LUSITANIA

BAETICA

NUMIDIA

A F R I C A
○

Small bronze city-coinages virtually cease under Tiberius (A.D. 14)

■ Gold
▲ Silver
△ Base silver
□ Brass
○ Bronze
♦ Copper

Note: Augustus reformed and enlarged the Roman imperial coinage, issuing gold, silver, brass and copper on an enormous scale

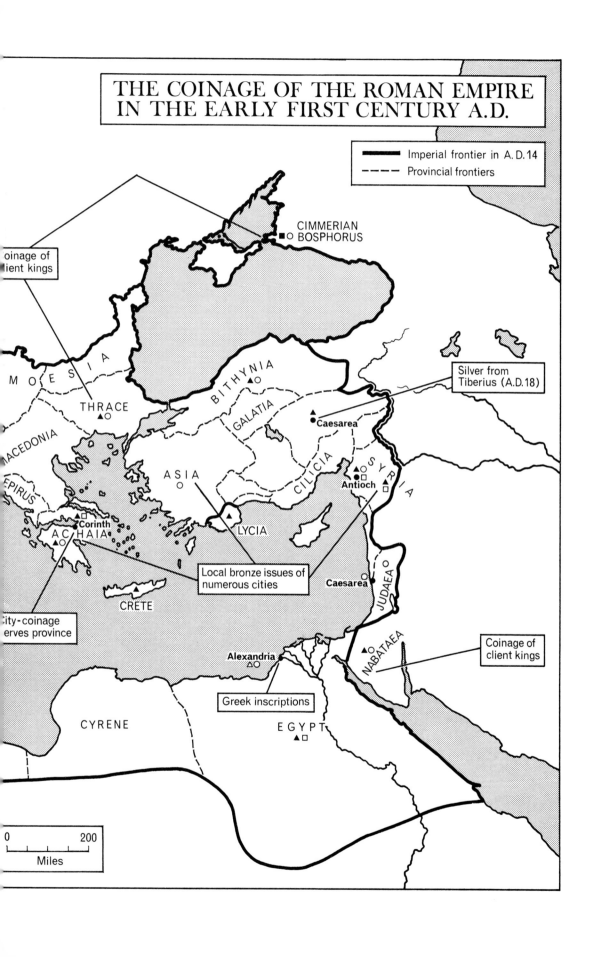

THE COINAGE OF THE ROMAN EMPIRE
IN THE EARLY FIRST CENTURY A.D.

▬▬▬▬	Imperial frontier in A.D. 14
- - - -	Provincial frontiers

CIMMERIAN
BOSPHORUS

Coinage of
client kings

Silver from
Tiberius (A.D. 18)

M O E S I A

THRACE

BITHYNIA

GALATIA

Caesarea

MACEDONIA

EPIRUS

ASIA

CILICIA

SYRIA

Antioch

Corinth

ACHAIA

LYCIA

Local bronze issues of
numerous cities

Caesarea

JUDAEA

City-coinage
serves province

CRETE

Coinage of
client kings

Alexandria

NABATAEA

Greek inscriptions

CYRENE

E G Y P T

0	200

Miles

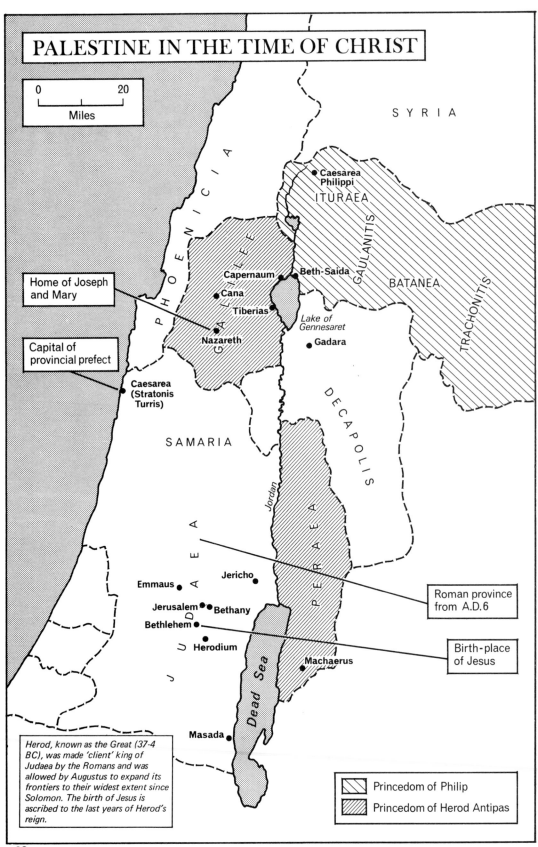

PALESTINE IN THE TIME OF CHRIST

0   20
Miles

SYRIA

Caesarea
Philippi

ITURAEA

GAULANITIS

BATANEA

TRACHONITIS

P H O E N I C I A

GALILEE

Capernaum

Beth-Saïda

Cana

Tiberias

Lake of
Gennesaret

Home of Joseph
and Mary

Nazareth

Gadara

DECAPOLIS

Capital of
provincial prefect

Caesarea
(Stratonis
Turris)

SAMARIA

Jordan

P E R A E A

J U D A E A

Emmaus

Jericho

Roman province
from A.D. 6

Jerusalem ● Bethany

Bethlehem

Herodium

Birth-place
of Jesus

Machaerus

Dead Sea

Masada

*Herod, known as the Great (37-4
BC), was made 'client' king of
Judaea by the Romans and was
allowed by Augustus to expand its
frontiers to their widest extent since
Solomon. The birth of Jesus is
ascribed to the last years of Herod's
reign.*

Princedom of Philip

Princedom of Herod Antipas

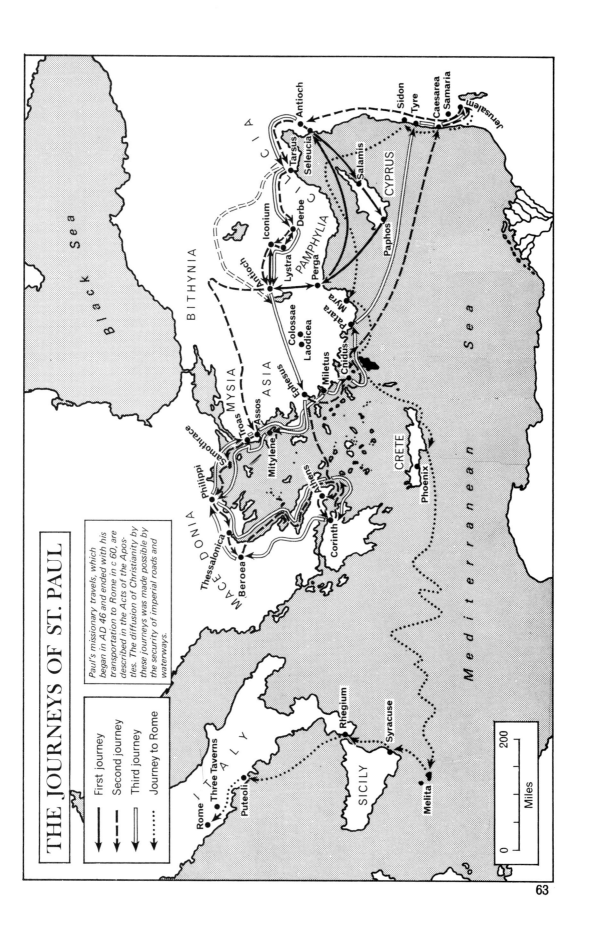

THE JOURNEYS OF ST. PAUL

Paul's missionary travels, which began in AD 46 and ended with his transportation to Rome in c 60, are described in the Acts of the Apostles. The diffusion of Christianity by these journeys was made possible by the security of imperial roads and waterways.

First journey
Second journey
Third journey
Journey to Rome

Miles
0   200

Black Sea

Mediterranean Sea

BITHYNIA

MYSIA

ASIA

MACEDONIA

PAMPHYLIA

CYPRUS

CRETE

SICILY

ITALY

Jerusalem
Samaria
Caesarea
Tyre
Sidon
Antioch
Tarsus
Seleucia
Salamis
Paphos
Perga
Myra
Patara
Cnidus
Miletus
Ephesus
Colossae
Laodicea
Derbe
Iconium
Lystra
Antioch
Assos
Troas
Mitylene
Samothrace
Philippi
Thessalonica
Beroea
Athens
Corinth
Phoenix
Rome
Three Taverns
Puteoli
Rhegium
Syracuse
Melita

63

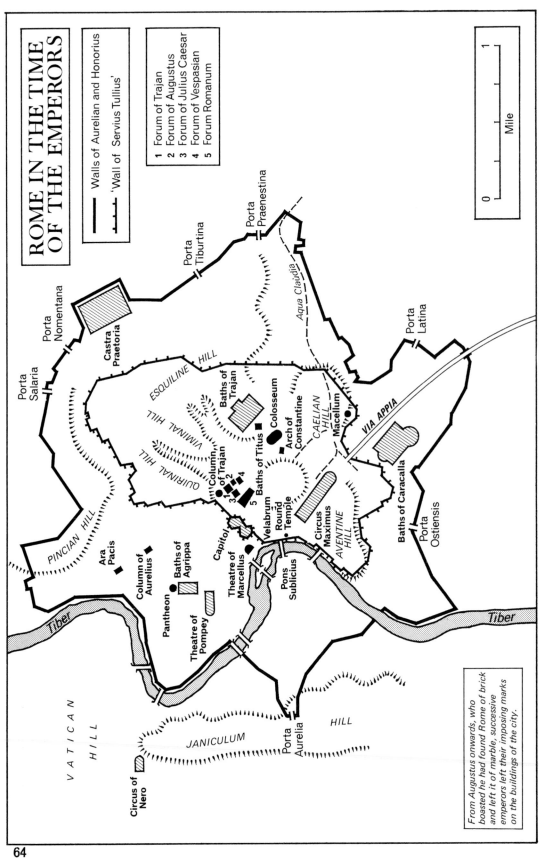

ROME IN THE TIME OF THE EMPERORS

Walls of Aurelian and Honorius
'Wall of Servius Tullius'

1 Forum of Trajan
2 Forum of Augustus
3 Forum of Julius Caesar
4 Forum of Vespasian
5 Forum Romanum

0 — Mile — 1

Porta Praenestina

Porta Tiburtina

Porta Nomentana

Castra Praetoria

Porta Salaria

ESQUILINE HILL

VIMINAL HILL

Baths of Trajan

Colosseum

Arch of Constantine

CAELIAN HILL

Macellum

VIA APPIA

Porta Latina

Aqua Claudia

QUIRINAL HILL

Column of Trajan

Baths of Titus

1 2 3 4 5

Velabrum

Round Temple

Circus Maximus

AVENTINE HILL

Baths of Caracalla

Porta Ostiensis

PINCIAN HILL

Ara Pacis

Column of Aurelius

Pantheon

Baths of Agrippa

Theatre of Pompey

Capitol

Theatre of Marcellus

Pons Sublicius

Tiber

Tiber

VATICAN HILL

Circus of Nero

JANICULUM HILL

Porta Aurelia

From Augustus onwards, who boasted he had found Rome of brick and left it of marble, successive emperors left their imposing marks on the buildings of the city.

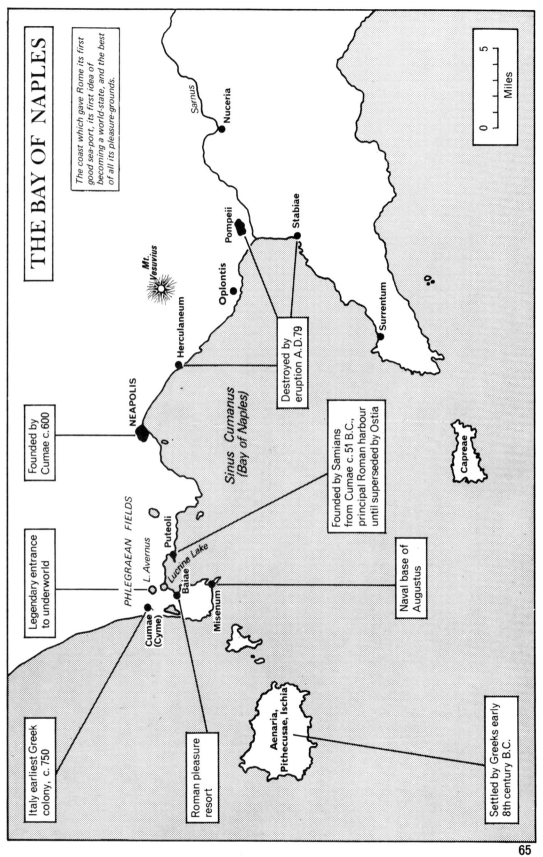

THE BAY OF NAPLES

The coast which gave Rome its first good sea-port, its first idea of becoming a world-state, and the best of all its pleasure-grounds.

Sarnus

Nuceria

Pompeii

Oplontis

Mt. Vesuvius

Stabiae

Herculaneum

Surrentum

Destroyed by eruption A.D. 79

NEAPOLIS

Sinus Cumanus (Bay of Naples)

Founded by Cumae c. 600

Capreae

Founded by Samians from Cumae c. 51 B.C., principal Roman harbour until superseded by Ostia

PHLEGRAEAN FIELDS

L. Avernus

Puteoli

Lucrine Lake

Baiae

Legendary entrance to underworld

Cumae (Cyme)

Misenum

Naval base of Augustus

Italy earliest Greek colony, c. 750

Roman pleasure resort

Aenaria, Pithecusae, Ischia

Settled by Greeks early 8th century B.C.

0   5
Miles

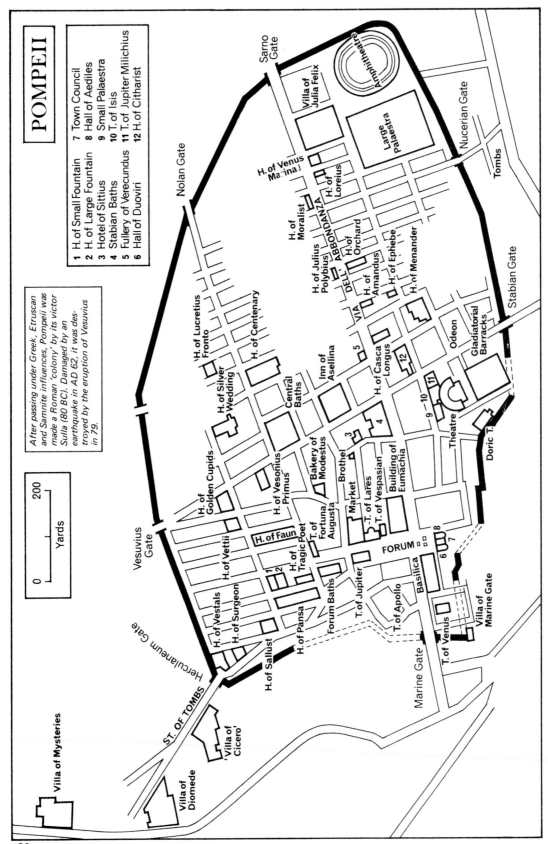

POMPEII

1 H. of Small Fountain
2 H. of Large Fountain
3 Hotel of Sittius
4 Stabian Baths
5 Fullery of Verecundus
6 Hall of Duoviri
7 Town Council
8 Hall of Aediles
9 Small Palaestra
10 T. of Isis
11 T. of Jupiter Milichius
12 H. of Citharist

After passing under Greek, Etruscan and Samnite influences, Pompeii was made a Roman 'colony' by its victor Sulla (80 BC). Damaged by an earthquake in AD 62, it was destroyed by the eruption of Vesuvius in 79.

0   200

Yards

Villa of Mysteries

Villa of Diomede

'Villa of Cicero'

ST. OF TOMBS

Herculaneum Gate

Vesuvius Gate

Nolan Gate

Sarno Gate

Amphitheatre

Villa of Julia Felix

Large Palaestra

Nucerian Gate

Tombs

H. of Venus Marina

H. of Loreius

DELL' ABBONDANZA

H. of Moralist

H. of Julius Polybius

H. of Orchard

H. of Amandus

VIA

H. of Ephebe

H. of Menander

H. of Lucretius Fronto

H. of Centenary

H. of Silver Wedding

H. of Golden Cupids

H. of Vesonius Primus

Central Baths

Inn of Asellina

H. of Casca Longus

Stabian Gate

Odeon

Gladiatorial Barracks

Theatre

Doric T.

Bakery of Modestus

Brothel

Market

T. of Lares

T. of Vespasian

Building of Eumachia

FORUM

Basilica

H. of Faun

T. of Fortuna Augusta

H. of Tragic Poet

H. of Vettii

H. of Vestals

H. of Surgeon

H. of Pansa

Forum Baths

H. of Sallust

T. of Jupiter

T. of Apollo

T. of Venus

Villa of Marine Gate

Marine Gate

66

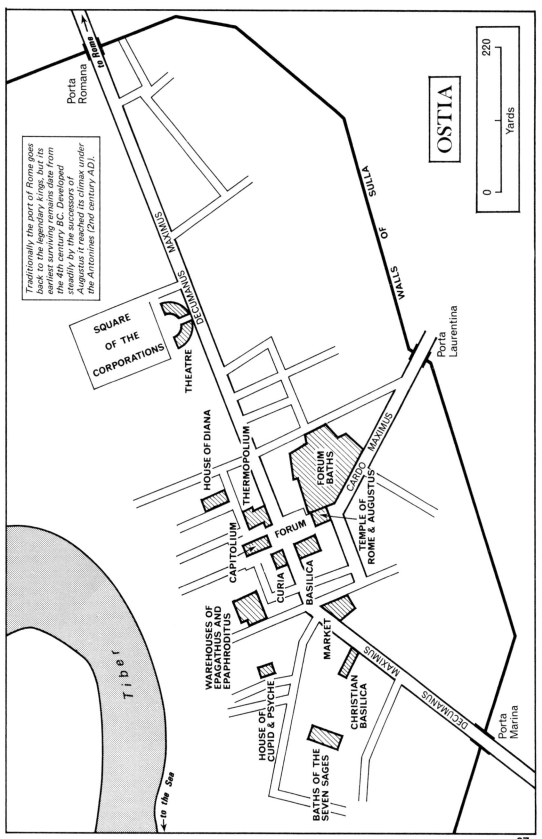

OSTIA

Traditionally the port of Rome goes back to the legendary kings, but its earliest surviving remains date from the 4th century BC. Developed steadily by the successors of Augustus it reached its climax under the Antonines (2nd century AD).

Porta Romana

to Rome

WALLS OF SULLA

Porta Laurentina

SQUARE OF THE CORPORATIONS

THEATRE

DECUMANUS MAXIMUS

HOUSE OF DIANA

THERMOPOLIUM

FORUM BATHS

CAPITOLIUM

FORUM

CARDO MAXIMUS

CURIA

BASILICA

TEMPLE OF ROME & AUGUSTUS

WAREHOUSES OF EPAGATHUS AND EPAPHRODITUS

MARKET

HOUSE OF CUPID & PSYCHE

CHRISTIAN BASILICA

DECUMANUS MAXIMUS

BATHS OF THE SEVEN SAGES

Porta Marina

Tiber

to the Sea

0   220

Yards

67

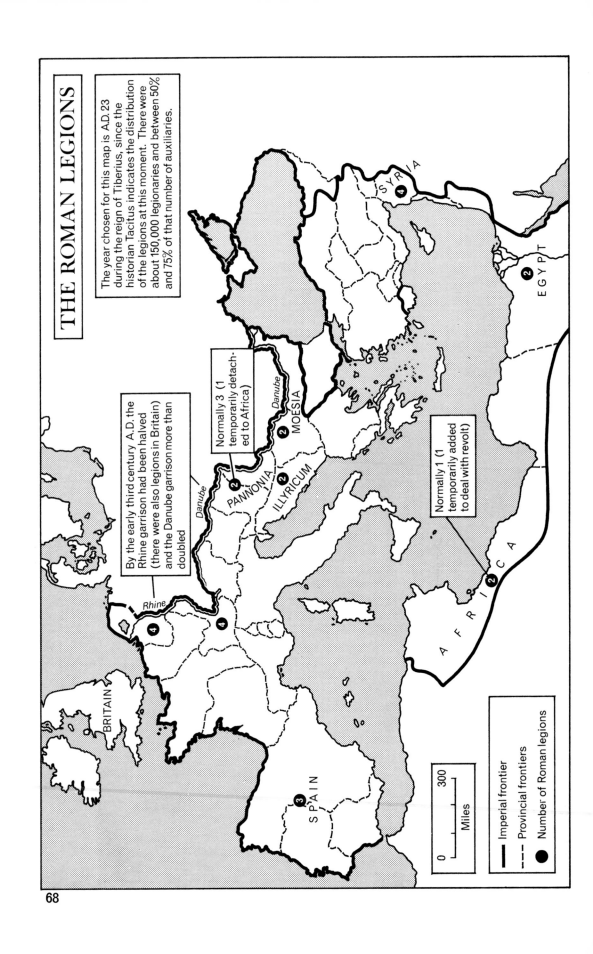

THE ROMAN LEGIONS

The year chosen for this map is A.D. 23 during the reign of Tiberius, since the historian Tacitus indicates the distribution of the legions at this moment. There were about 150,000 legionaries and between 50% and 75% of that number of auxiliaries.

By the early third century A.D. the Rhine garrison had been halved (there were also legions in Britain) and the Danube garrison more than doubled

Normally 3 (1 temporarily detached to Africa)

Normally 1 (1 temporarily added to deal with revolt)

BRITAIN

Rhine

Danube

Danube

Danube

PANNONIA

ILLYRICUM

MOESIA

SPAIN

A F R I C A

E G Y P T

S Y R I A

Imperial frontier
Provincial frontiers
Number of Roman legions

0   300
Miles

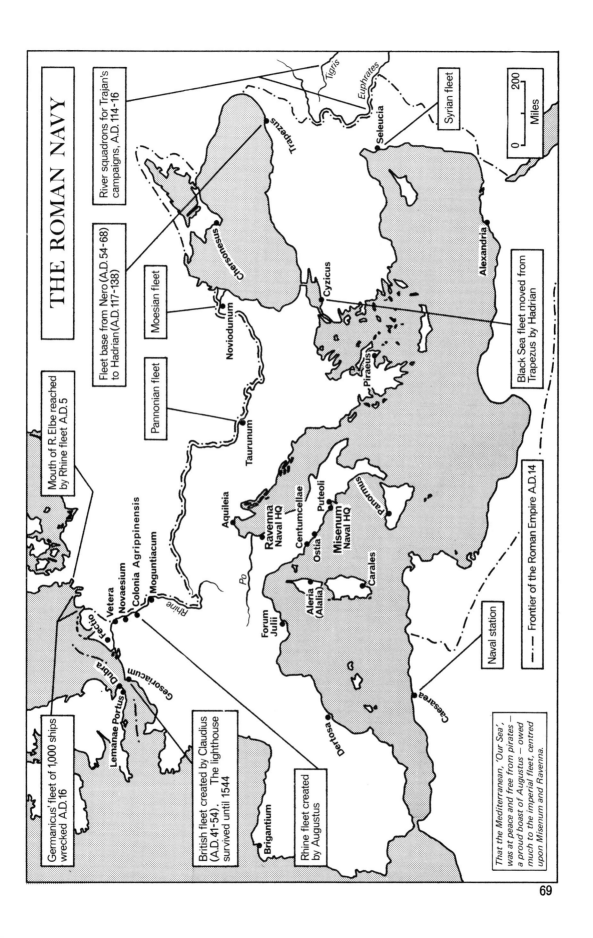

THE ROMAN NAVY

River squadrons for Trajan's campaigns, A.D. 114-16

Fleet base from Nero (A.D. 54-68) to Hadrian (A.D. 117-138)

Moesian fleet

Pannonian fleet

Mouth of R. Elbe reached by Rhine fleet A.D. 5

Syrian fleet

Black Sea fleet moved from Trapezus by Hadrian

Naval station

—·—·— Frontier of the Roman Empire A.D. 14

Germanicus' fleet of 1,000 ships wrecked A.D. 16

British fleet created by Claudius (A.D. 41-54). The lighthouse survived until 1544

Rhine fleet created by Augustus

That the Mediterranean, 'Our Sea', was at peace and free from pirates — a proud boast of Augustus — owed much to the imperial fleet, centred upon Misenum and Ravenna.

Tigris

Euphrates

Seleucia

Trapezus

Alexandria

Chersonesus

Cyzicus

Noviodunum

Piraeus

Taurunum

Aquileia

Ravenna Naval HQ

Centumcellae

Puteoli

Ostia

Misenum Naval HQ

Pannonius

Carales

Aleria (Alalia)

Forum Julii

Dertosa

Caesarea

Vetera

Novaesium

Colonia Agrippinensis

Moguntiacum

Rhine

Po

Fectio

Dubris

Gesoriacum

Lemanae Portus

Brigantium

0   200
Miles

69

BRITANNIA (AD 71)
(AD 59)
(AD 43–47)
Londinium

LOWER GERMANY
Colonia Agrippinensis

FREE GERMANY

Rhine
Moguntiacum
AGRI DECUMAT (83)

LUGDUNENSIS

GALLIA

UPPER GERMANY

RHAETIA

NORICUM

Danube

PANNONIA
UPPER
LOWER

Lugdunum

AQUITANIA

NARBONENSIS

Aquileia

ILLYRICUM

Nemausus

ITALIA

Adriatic Sea

TARRACONENSIS

Tarraco

Rome

HISPANIA

LUSITANIA

SARDINIA

BAETICA

Corduba
Gades

SICILY

Carthage

MAURETANIA (A.D. 42)

AFRICA

– – – Frontier of Roman Empire A.D. 14
– · – · Frontier of Roman Empire A.D. 117
· · · · · Province boundaries

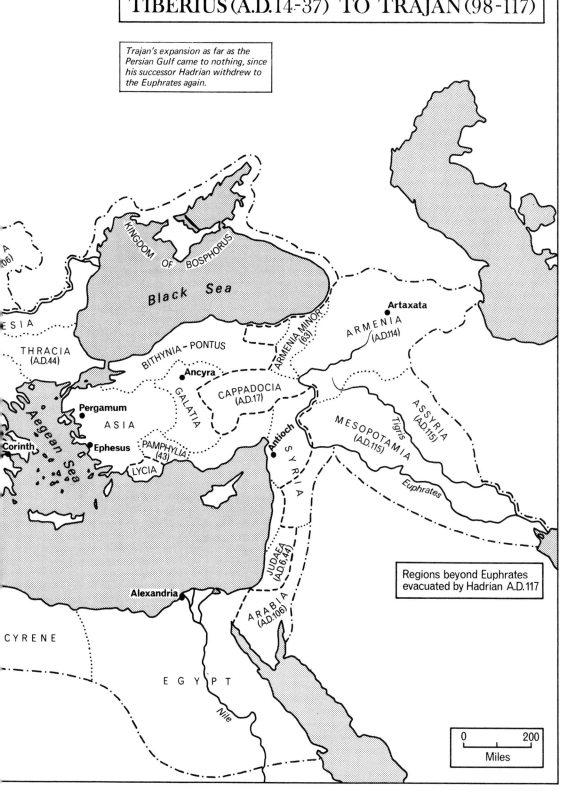

THE ROMAN EMPIRE FROM TIBERIUS (A.D.14-37) TO TRAJAN (98-117)

Trajan's expansion as far as the Persian Gulf came to nothing, since his successor Hadrian withdrew to the Euphrates again.

KINGDOM OF BOSPHORUS

Black Sea

Artaxata

ARMENIA MINOR (63)

ARMENIA (A.D.114)

THRACIA (A.D.44)

BITHYNIA - PONTUS

Ancyra

CAPPADOCIA (A.D.17)

ASSYRIA (AD.115)

Tigris

MESOPOTAMIA (A.D.115)

GALATIA

Pergamum

ASIA

PAMPHYLIA (43)

Antioch

S Y R I A

Euphrates

Corinth

Ephesus

LYCIA

Aegean Sea

JUDAEA (AD.6,44)

Regions beyond Euphrates evacuated by Hadrian A.D.117

Alexandria

ARABIA (A.D.106)

CYRENE

E G Y P T

Nile

0   200

Miles

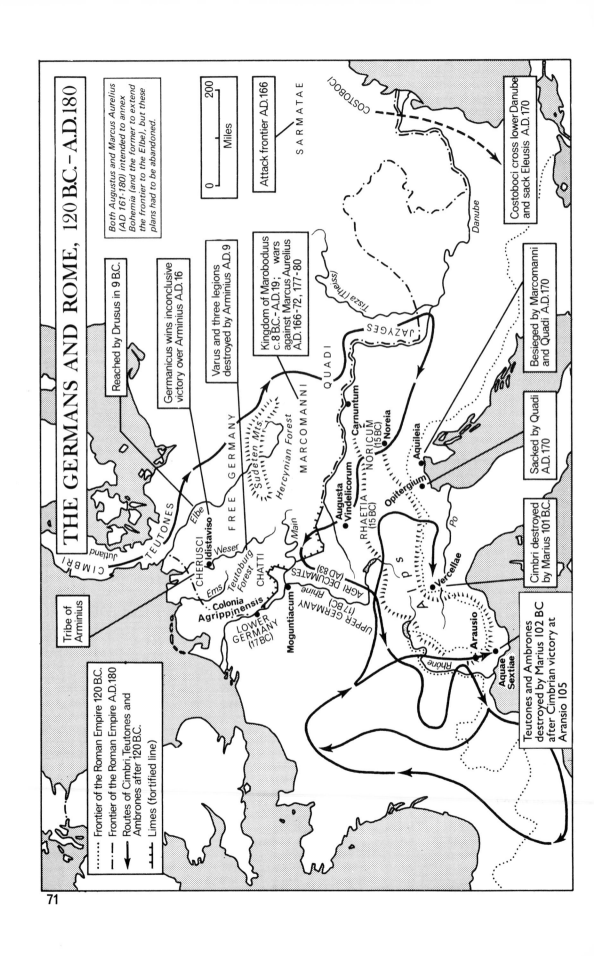

THE GERMANS AND ROME, 120 B.C.–A.D.180

Both Augustus and Marcus Aurelius (AD 161-180) intended to annex Bohemia (and the former to the Elbe), but these plans had to be abandoned.

Attack frontier A.D.166

Costoboci cross lower Danube and sack Eleusis A.D.170

Reached by Drusus in 9 B.C.

Germanicus wins inconclusive victory over Arminius A.D.16

Varus and three legions destroyed by Arminius A.D.9

Kingdom of Maroboduus c.8 B.C.-A.D.19; wars against Marcus Aurelius A.D.166-72, 177-80

Tribe of Arminius

Besieged by Marcomanni and Quadi A.D.170

Sacked by Quadi A.D.170

Cimbri destroyed by Marius 101 B.C.

Teutones and Ambrones destroyed by Marius 102 BC after Cimbrian victory at Aransio 105

SARMATAE

COSTOBOCI

Danube

Tisza (Theiss)

JAZYGES

QUADI

MARCOMANNI

Hercynian Forest

Sudeten Mts.

FREE GERMANY

Elbe

Weser

Ems

CHERUSCI
• Idistaviso

Teutoburg Forest

CHATTI

TEUTONES

CIMBRI

Jutland

Colonia
Agrippinensis

LOWER GERMANY (17BC)

Moguntiacum

Rhine

AGRI DECUMATES (AD 83)

UPPER GERMANY (17BC)

Main

Augusta
• Vindelicorum

RHAETIA (15BC)

NORICUM (15BC)

Carnuntum

• Noreia

Opitergium

Aquileia

A L P S

Po

• Vercellae

Rhone

Arausio

Aquae
Sextiae

Frontier of the Roman Empire 120 B.C.

Frontier of the Roman Empire A.D.180

Routes of Cimbri,Teutones and Ambrones after 120 B.C.

Limes (fortified line)

200

0

Miles

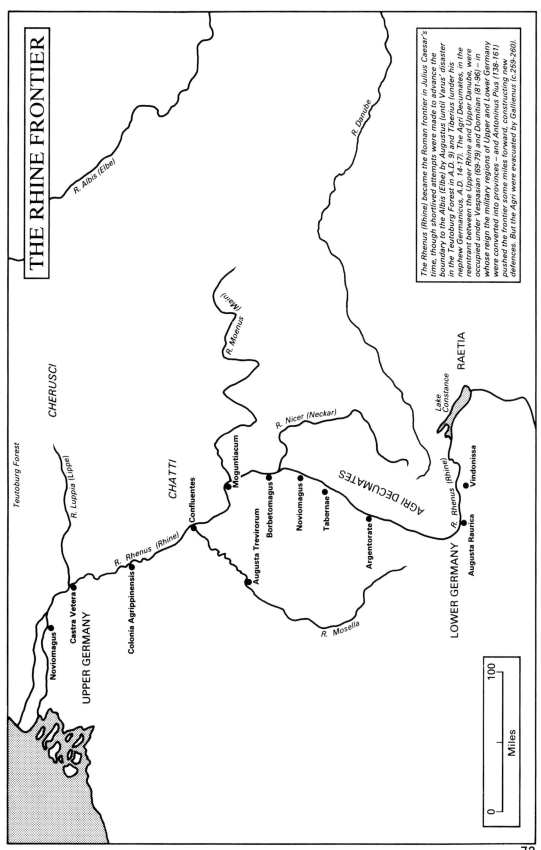

THE RHINE FRONTIER

The Rhenus (Rhine) became the Roman frontier in Julius Caesar's time, though shortlived attempts were made to advance the boundary to the Albis (Elbe) by Augustus (until Varus' disaster in the Teutoburg Forest in A.D. 9) and Tiberius (under his nephew Germanicus, A.D. 14-17). The Agri Decumates, in the reentrant between the Upper Rhine and Upper Danube, were occupied under Vespasian (69-79) and Domitian (81-96) – in whose reign the military regions of Upper and Lower Germany were converted into provinces – and Antoninus Pius (138-161) pushed the frontier some miles forward, constructing new defences. But the Agri were evacuated by Gallienus (c.259-260).

CHERUSCI

Teutoburg Forest

R. Albis (Elbe)

R. Danube

R. Moenus (Main)

R. Luppia (Lippe)

R. Nicer (Neckar)

CHATTI

Moguntiacum

Confluentes

Borbetomagus

Noviomagus

Tabernae

Augusta Trevirorum

Argentorate

AGRI DECUMATES

Lake Constance

RAETIA

R. Rhenus (Rhine)

Vindonissa

Augusta Raurica

R. Rhenus (Rhine)

LOWER GERMANY

R. Mosella

Colonia Agrippinensis

Castra Vetera

Noviomagus

UPPER GERMANY

0   100

Miles

72

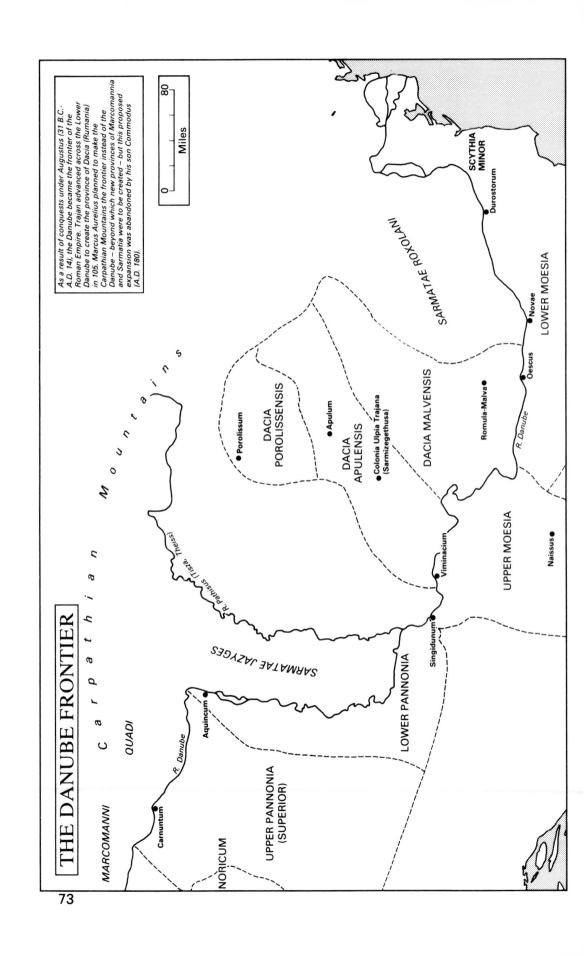

THE DANUBE FRONTIER

As a result of conquests under Augustus (31 B.C.-A.D. 14), the Danube became the frontier of the Roman Empire. Trajan advanced across the Lower Danube to create the province of Dacia (Rumania) in 105. Marcus Aurelius planned to make the Carpathian Mountains the frontier instead of the Danube – beyond which new provinces of Marcomannia and Sarmatia were to be created – but this proposed expansion was abandoned by his son Commodus (A.D. 180).

0   80
Miles

MARCOMANNI

QUADI

C a r p a t h i a n   M o u n t a i n s

NORICUM

UPPER PANNONIA (SUPERIOR)

Carnuntum

R. Danube

Aquincum

R. Parthisus (Tisza, Theiss)

SARMATAE JAZYGES

LOWER PANNONIA

Singidunum

Viminacium

UPPER MOESIA

Naissus

DACIA POROLISSENSIS

Porolissum

Apulum

DACIA APULENSIS

Colonia Ulpia Trajana (Sarmizegethusa)

DACIA MALVENSIS

Romula-Malva

Oescus

R. Danube

Novae

LOWER MOESIA

Durostorum

SCYTHIA MINOR

SARMATAE ROXOLANI

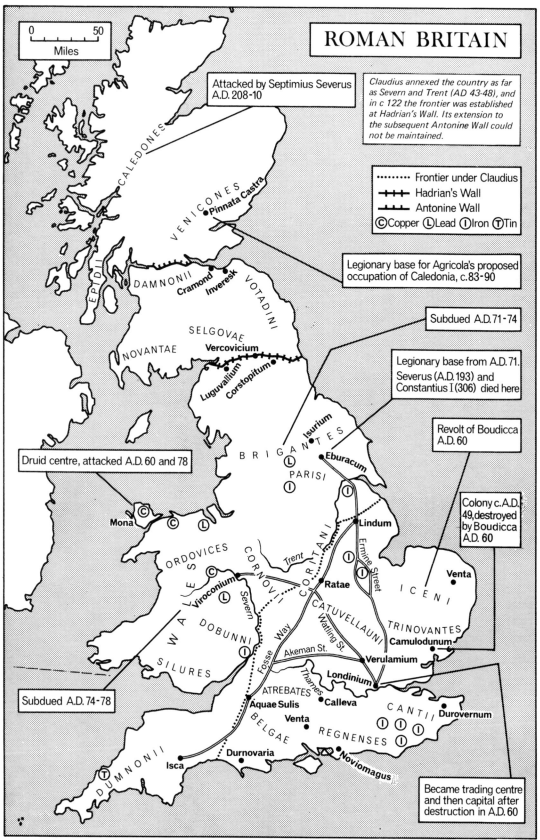

ROMAN BRITAIN

Claudius annexed the country as far as Severn and Trent (AD 43-48), and in c 122 the frontier was established at Hadrian's Wall. Its extension to the subsequent Antonine Wall could not be maintained.

········· Frontier under Claudius
━┼━┼━ Hadrian's Wall
━┴━┴━ Antonine Wall
ⒸCopper ⒧Lead ⒤Iron ⓉTin

Attacked by Septimius Severus A.D. 208-10

Legionary base for Agricola's proposed occupation of Caledonia, c.83-90

Subdued A.D. 71-74

Legionary base from A.D. 71. Severus (A.D. 193) and Constantius I (306) died here

Revolt of Boudicca A.D. 60

Druid centre, attacked A.D. 60 and 78

Colony c.A.D. 49, destroyed by Boudicca A.D. 60

Subdued A.D. 74-78

Became trading centre and then capital after destruction in A.D. 60

CALEDONES

VENICONES
Pinnata Castra

EPIDII

DAMNONII
Cramond Inveresk

VOTADINI

NOVANTAE

SELGOVAE
Vercovicium

Luguvallium Corstopitum

BRIGANTES
Isurium
Ⓛ •Eburacum
PARISI
ⓘ

Mona Ⓒ Ⓒ Ⓛ

ORDOVICES
Ⓒ
Viroconium Ⓛ
Severn

CORNOVII

CORITANI
Trent
•Lindum
Ermine Street
ⓘ
ⓘ
•Ratae

ICENI
•Venta

WALES

DOBUNNI
ⓘ

CATUVELLAUNI
Watling St.
Akeman St.
Verulamium•

TRINOVANTES
Camulodunum•

SILURES

Fosse Way

Thames
Londinium•

ATREBATES
Aquae Sulis
Venta• •Calleva

CANTII
•Durovernum

BELGAE
REGNENSES
ⓘ ⓘ ⓘ
ⓘ

DUMNONII
Ⓣ
Isca• •Durnovaria
•Noviomagus

0   50
Miles

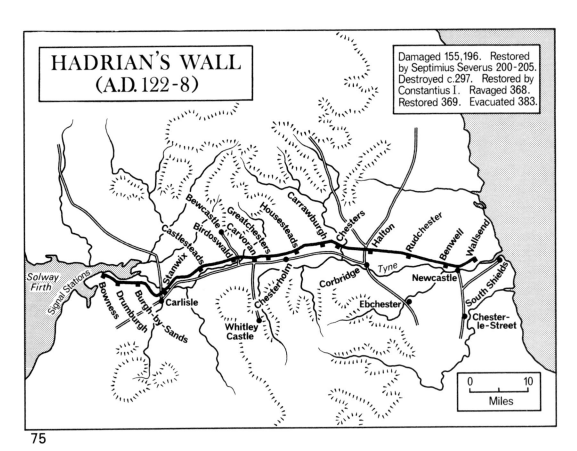

HADRIAN'S WALL
(A.D. 122-8)

Damaged 155,196. Restored by Septimius Severus 200-205. Destroyed c.297. Restored by Constantius I. Ravaged 368. Restored 369. Evacuated 383.

Carrawburgh

Bewcastle
Greatchesters
Housesteads
Chesters
Halton
Rudchester
Benwell
Wallsend

Castlesteads
Birdoswald
Carvoran
Carrawburgh

Stanwix

Solway Firth

Signal Stations

Bowness
Drumburgh

Burgh-by-Sands
Carlisle

Chesterholm

Corbridge
Tyne
Newcastle

Whitley Castle

Ebchester

South Shields

Chester-le-Street

0   10
Miles

75

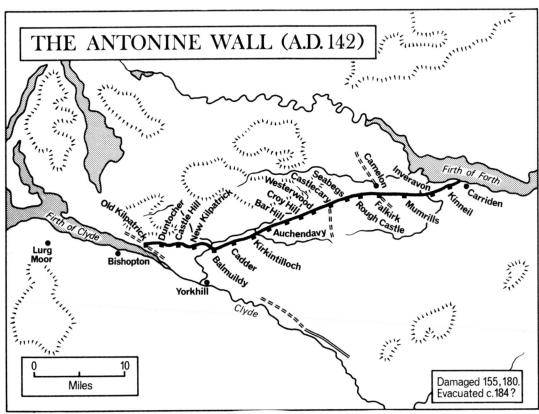

THE ANTONINE WALL (A.D. 142)

Firth of Forth

Camelon
Inveravon
Carriden

Seabegs
Castlecary
Westerwood
Croy Hill
Bar Hill
Kinneil

Old Kilpatrick
Duntocher
Castle Hill
New Kilpatrick

Falkirk
Mumrills
Rough Castle

Firth of Clyde

Auchendavy

Lurg Moor

Bishopton

Cadder
Kirkintilloch

Balmuildy

Yorkhill

Clyde

0   10
Miles

Damaged 155,180. Evacuated c.184?

76

THE WORLD ACCORDING TO PTOLEMY, c. A.D. 150

The Geography of Claudius Ptolemaeus of Alexandria, including an atlas, showed awareness of the existence of China, but not of its shape.

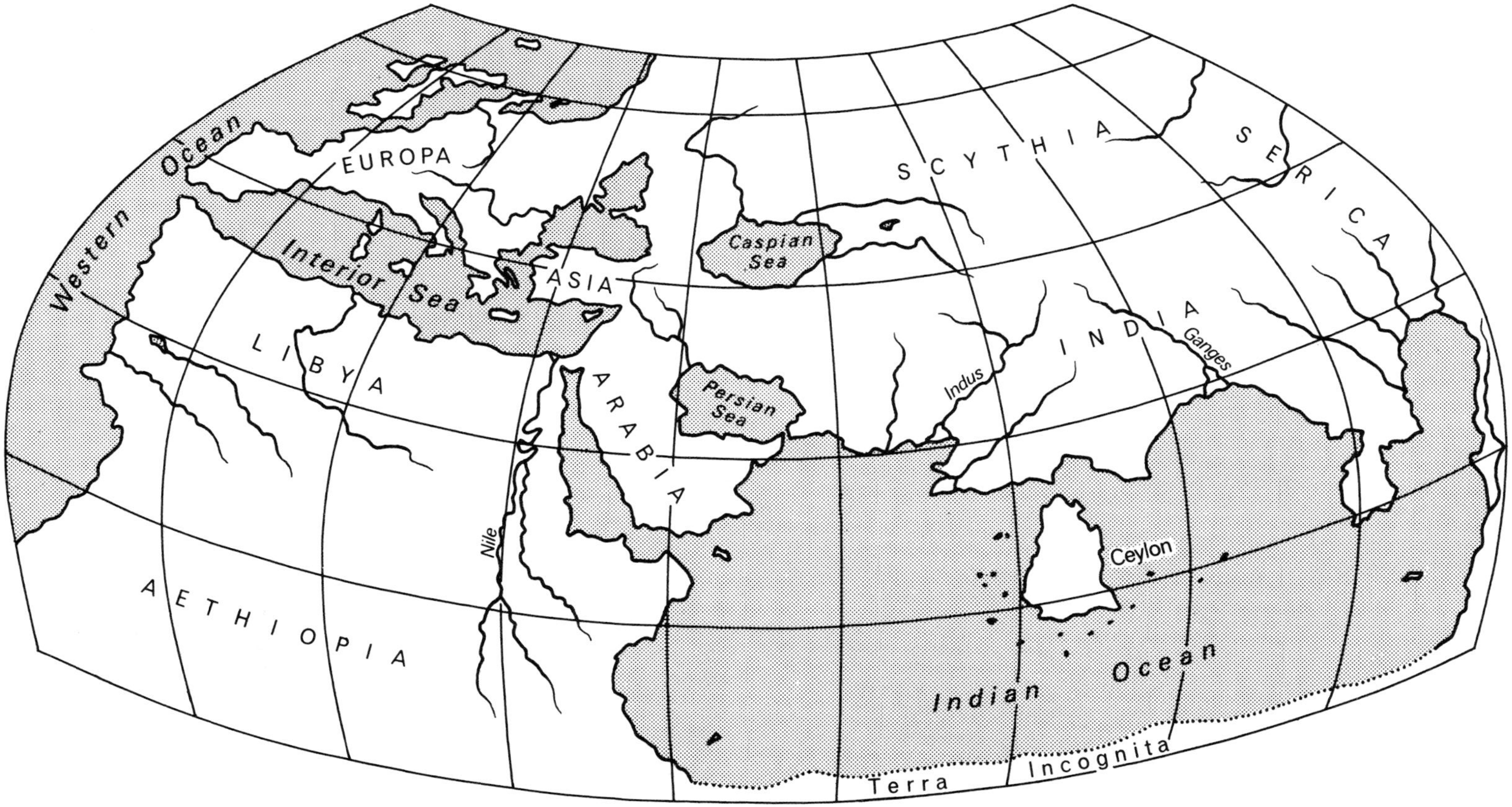

SERICA

SCYTHIA

INDIA

Ganges

Indus

Ceylon

Indian Ocean

Terra Incognita

Caspian Sea

Persian Sea

ARABIA

ASIA

EUROPA

Interior Sea

Nile

LIBYA

AETHIOPIA

Western Ocean

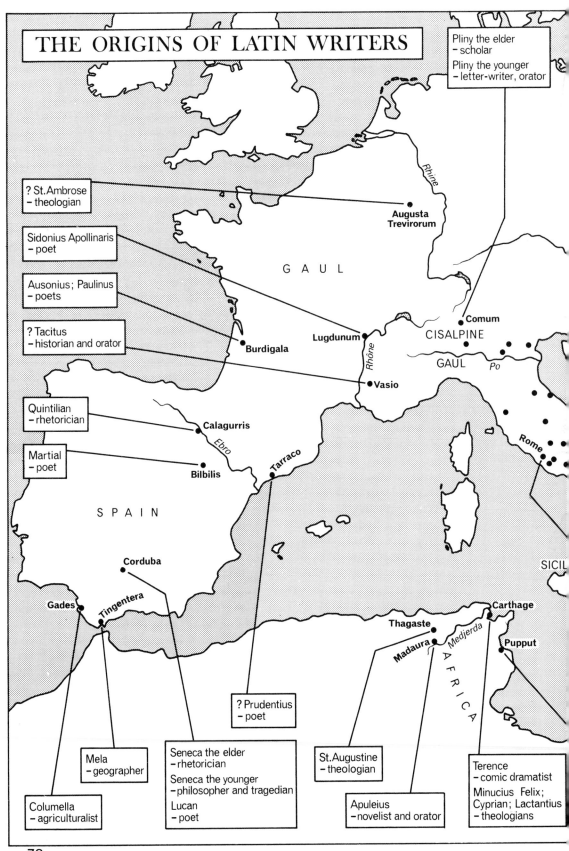

THE ORIGINS OF LATIN WRITERS

Pliny the elder
– scholar
Pliny the younger
– letter-writer, orator

? St. Ambrose
– theologian

Sidonius Apollinaris
– poet

Ausonius; Paulinus
– poets

? Tacitus
– historian and orator

Quintilian
– rhetorician

Martial
– poet

Mela
– geographer

Columella
– agriculturalist

Seneca the elder
– rhetorician
Seneca the younger
– philosopher and tragedian
Lucan
– poet

? Prudentius
– poet

St. Augustine
– theologian

Apuleius
– novelist and orator

Terence
– comic dramatist
Minucius Felix;
Cyprian; Lactantius
– theologians

Rhine

Augusta
Trevirorum

GAUL

Comum

CISALPINE

GAUL   Po

Lugdunum

Rhône

Burdigala

Vasio

Rome

Calagurris

Ebro

Tarraco

Bilbilis

SPAIN

Corduba

SICIL

Gades

Tingentera

Carthage

Thagaste

Medjerda

Pupput

Madaura

A F R I C A

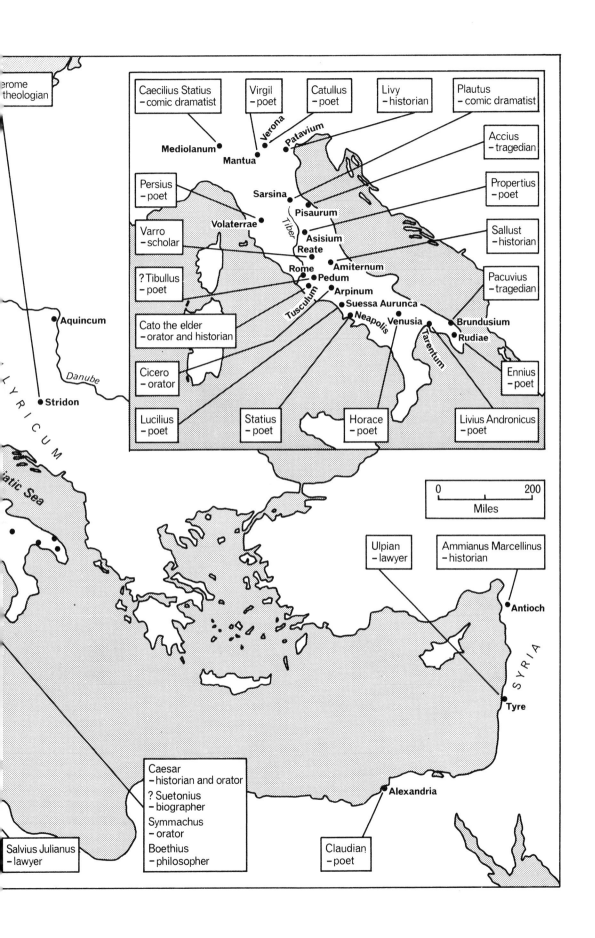

Jerome
– theologian

Caecilius Statius
– comic dramatist

Virgil
– poet

Catullus
– poet

Livy
– historian

Plautus
– comic dramatist

Accius
– tragedian

Persius
– poet

Propertius
– poet

Varro
– scholar

Sallust
– historian

?Tibullus
– poet

Pacuvius
– tragedian

Cato the elder
– orator and historian

Cicero
– orator

Ennius
– poet

Lucilius
– poet

Statius
– poet

Horace
– poet

Livius Andronicus
– poet

Mediolanum

Verona

Patavium

Mantua

Sarsina

Pisaurum

Volaterrae

Asisium

Reate

Amiternum

Rome

Pedum

Arpinum

Tusculum

Suessa Aurunca

Neapolis

Venusia

Brundusium

Rudiae

Tarentum

Tiber

Aquincum

Danube

Stridon

ILLYRICUM

Adriatic Sea

0 — 200
Miles

Ulpian
– lawyer

Ammianus Marcellinus
– historian

Antioch

SYRIA

Tyre

Caesar
– historian and orator
?Suetonius
– biographer
Symmachus
– orator
Boethius
– philosopher

Salvius Julianus
– lawyer

Alexandria

Claudian
– poet

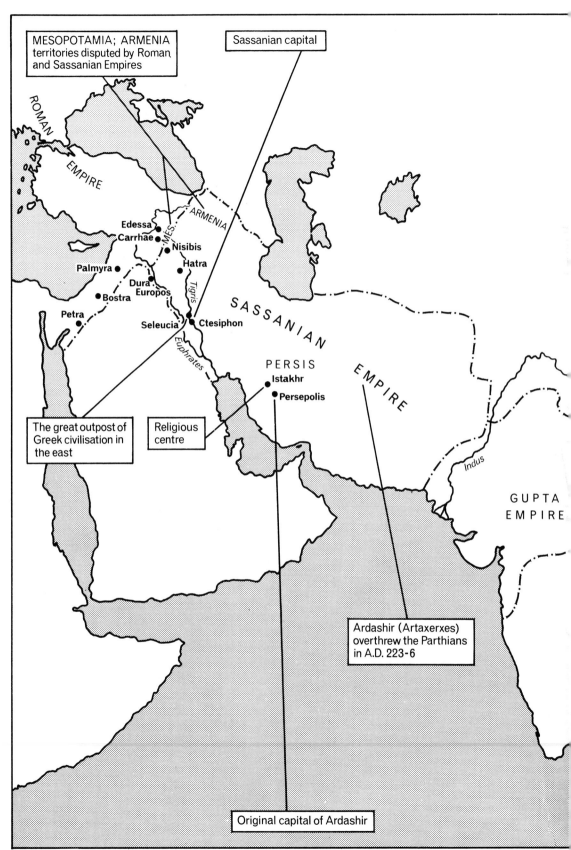

MESOPOTAMIA; ARMENIA
territories disputed by Roman
and Sassanian Empires

Sassanian capital

ROMAN

EMPIRE

ARMENIA

MES.

Edessa
Carrhae
Nisibis
Hatra
Palmyra
Dura
Europos
Bostra

Tigris

Petra

Seleucia
Ctesiphon

Euphrates

SASSANIAN

EMPIRE

PERSIS

Istakhr
Persepolis

The great outpost of
Greek civilisation in
the east

Religious
centre

Indus

GUPTA
EMPIRE

Ardashir (Artaxerxes)
overthrew the Parthians
in A.D. 223-6

Original capital of Ardashir

79

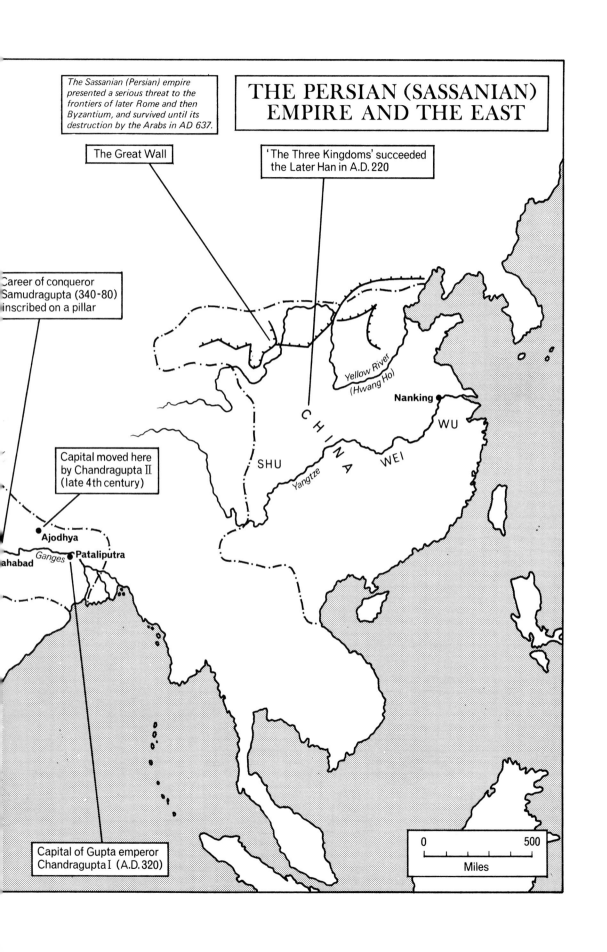

THE PERSIAN (SASSANIAN) EMPIRE AND THE EAST

The Great Wall

'The Three Kingdoms' succeeded the Later Han in A.D. 220

Career of conqueror Samudragupta (340-80) inscribed on a pillar

Capital moved here by Chandragupta II (late 4th century)

Yellow River (Hwang Ho)

Nanking

C H I N A

WU

SHU

Yangtze

WEI

Ajodhya

Ganges **Pataliputra**

ahabad

Capital of Gupta emperor Chandragupta I (A.D. 320)

0   500

Miles

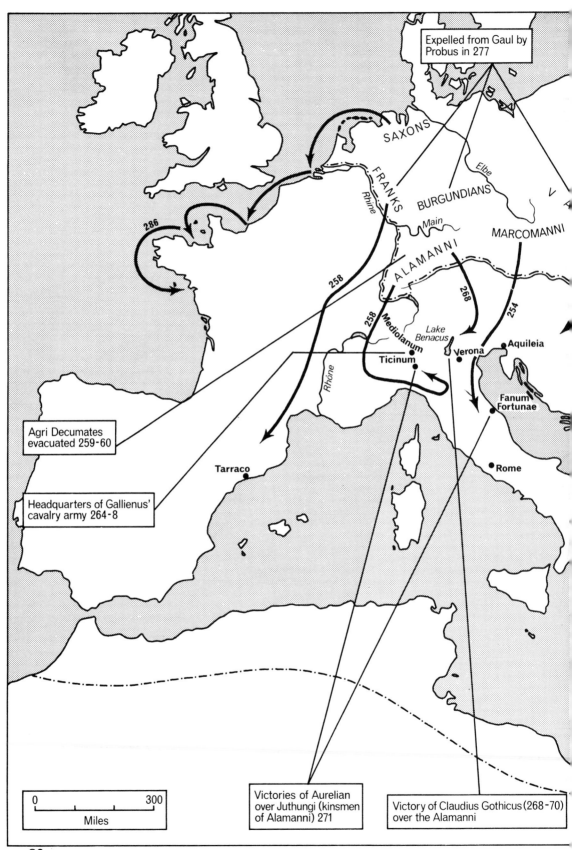

Expelled from Gaul by
Probus in 277

SAXONS

FRANKS

Rhine

BURGUNDIANS

Elbe

Main

MARCOMANNI

A L A M A N N I

286

258

258

268

254

Rhône

Mediolanum

Lake
Benacus

Ticinum

Verona

Aquileia

Fanum
Fortunae

Rome

Tarraco

Agri Decumates
evacuated 259-60

Headquarters of Gallienus'
cavalry army 264-8

Victories of Aurelian
over Juthungi (kinsmen
of Alamanni) 271

Victory of Claudius Gothicus (268-70)
over the Alamanni

0   300
Miles

GERMAN INVASIONS IN THE THIRD CENTURY A.D.

Evacuated c.271

First crossed the Danube under Severus Alexander (222-35

From the 230s until the 260s the Germans burst over the frontiers with ever increasing force, but then the dissolution of the empire was prevented by Gallienus, Claudius II Gothicus, Aurelian and Probus.

King lends fleet to raiders 254

Decius fell to Goths 251

Dnieper

Dniester

EAST GOTHS

HERULI

Cimmerian Bosphorus

Panticapaeum

L S

incum

DACIA

WEST GOTHS

ube

Abrittus

264

269

Marcianopolis

Black Sea

Naïssus

BITHYNIA

Trapezus

SASSANIAN

EMPIRE

Philippopolis

Byzantium

Chalcedon

Thessalonica

Pessinus

Ephesus

Sparta

Overrun by Goths 256

Victory of Gallienus over Goths 268

Captured by Goths from Decius (249-51)

Sacked by Goths in 253

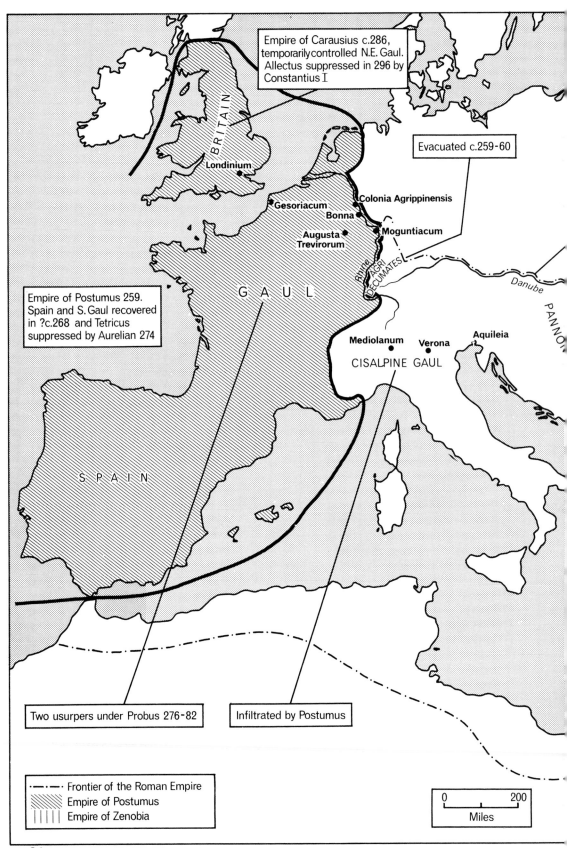

Empire of Carausius c.286, temporarily controlled N.E. Gaul. Allectus suppressed in 296 by Constantius I

Evacuated c.259-60

BRITAIN

Londinium

Gesoriacum

Colonia Agrippinensis

Bonna

Moguntiacum

Augusta
Trevirorum

Rhine

AGRI
DECUMATES

Danube

PANNON

Empire of Postumus 259. Spain and S. Gaul recovered in ?c.268 and Tetricus suppressed by Aurelian 274

G A U L

Mediolanum

Verona

Aquileia

CISALPINE GAUL

S P A I N

Two usurpers under Probus 276-82

Infiltrated by Postumus

—·—·— Frontier of the Roman Empire
////// Empire of Postumus
|||||| Empire of Zenobia

0   200

Miles

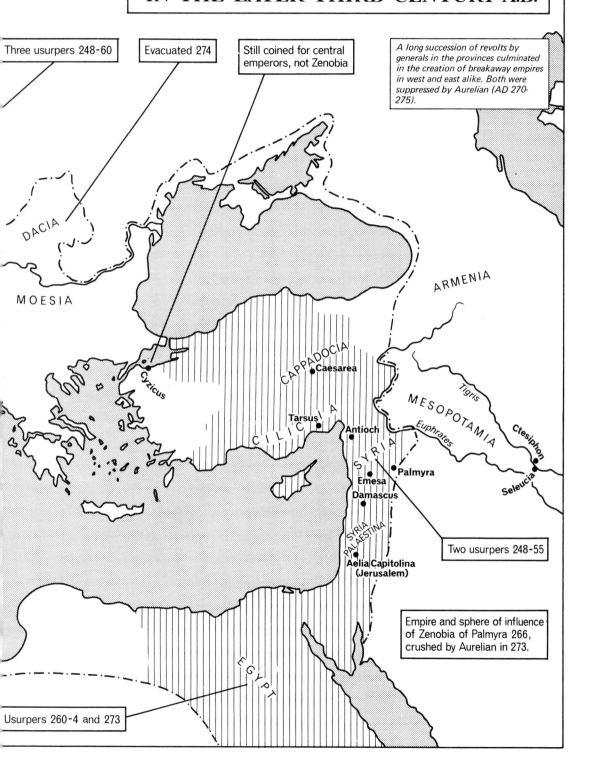

THE BREAKDOWN AND RECOVERY OF THE ROMAN EMPIRE IN THE LATER THIRD CENTURY A.D.

Three usurpers 248-60

Evacuated 274

Still coined for central emperors, not Zenobia

A long succession of revolts by generals in the provinces culminated in the creation of breakaway empires in west and east alike. Both were suppressed by Aurelian (AD 270-275).

DACIA

MOESIA

ARMENIA

CAPPADOCIA
Caesarea

Cyzicus

MESOPOTAMIA

Tigris

Ctesiphon

Tarsus

C I L I C I A

Antioch

Euphrates

Seleucia

S Y R I A

Palmyra

Emesa

Damascus

Two usurpers 248-55

SYRIA PALAESTINA

Aelia Capitolina
(Jerusalem)

Empire and sphere of influence of Zenobia of Palmyra 266, crushed by Aurelian in 273.

E G Y P T

Usurpers 260-4 and 273

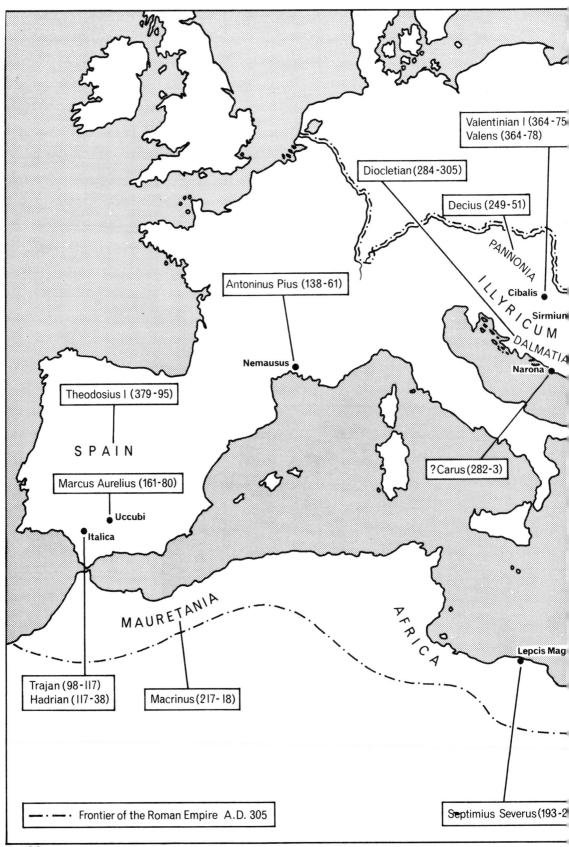

Valentinian I (364-75
Valens (364-78)

Diocletian (284-305)

Decius (249-51)

PANNONIA

ILLYRICUM

Cibalis

Sirmium

DALMATIA

Antoninus Pius (138-61)

Narona

Nemausus

Theodosius I (379-95)

S P A I N

?Carus (282-3)

Marcus Aurelius (161-80)

Uccubi

Italica

MAURETANIA

AFRICA

Lepcis Mag

Trajan (98-117)
Hadrian (117-38)

Macrinus (217-18)

— · — · Frontier of the Roman Empire A.D. 305

Septimius Severus (193-2

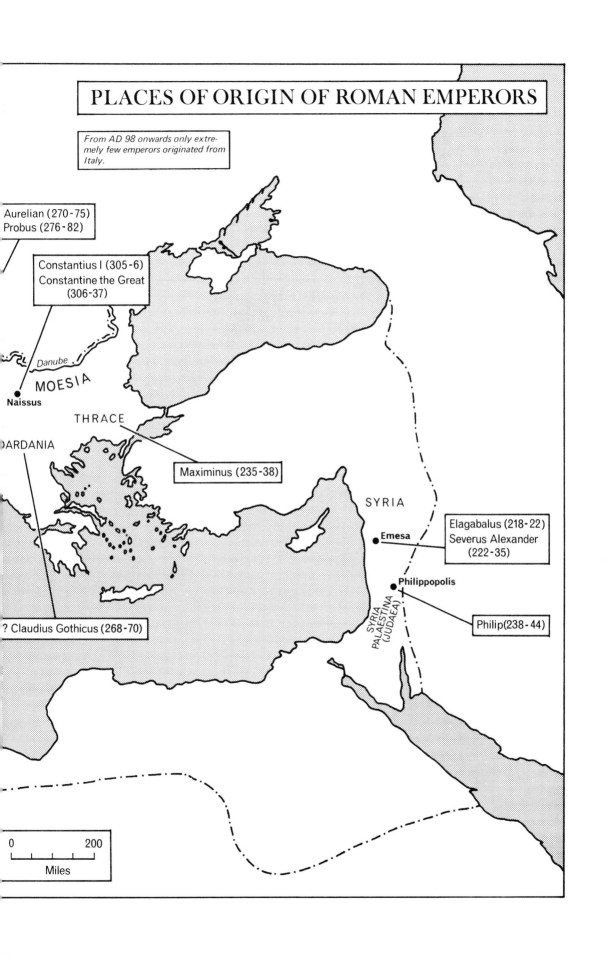

PLACES OF ORIGIN OF ROMAN EMPERORS

From AD 98 onwards only extremely few emperors originated from Italy.

Aurelian (270-75)
Probus (276-82)

Constantius I (305-6)
Constantine the Great
(306-37)

Danube

MOESIA

● Naissus

THRACE

DARDANIA

Maximinus (235-38)

SYRIA

● Emesa

Elagabalus (218-22)
Severus Alexander
(222-35)

● Philippopolis

SYRIA
PALAESTINA
(JUDAEA)

Philip(238-44)

? Claudius Gothicus (268-70)

0   200

Miles

GERMANIA

Colonia

Rhine

Regina

Aquincum

PANNONIA

Mursa

Lutetia

Genabum

Tergeste

Ravenna

DALMATIA

Vesontio

Alps

Genua

ITALY

APULIA

G A U L

Burdigala

CALAB

Tolosa

Rome

Pyrenees

Massilia

CAMPANIA

S P A I N

SARDINIA

Corduba

Jews deported from
Rome by Tiberius
A.D. 14 - 37

Caralis

Panormus

SICILY

Gades

Melita

Carthage

Volubilis

Atlas   Mountains

S A H A R A

Oea

0	250

Miles

■ Areas of widespread Jewish settlement

● Towns with large Jewish communities

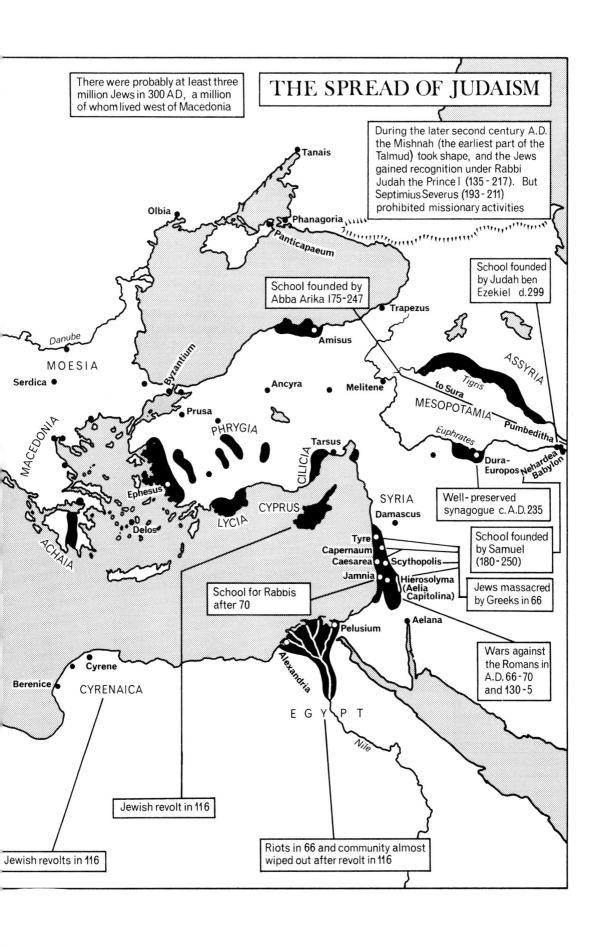

THE SPREAD OF JUDAISM

There were probably at least three million Jews in 300 A.D., a million of whom lived west of Macedonia

During the later second century A.D. the Mishnah (the earliest part of the Talmud) took shape, and the Jews gained recognition under Rabbi Judah the Prince I (135 - 217). But Septimius Severus (193 - 211) prohibited missionary activities

School founded by Judah ben Ezekiel d.299

School founded by Abba Arika 175-247

Tanais

Olbia

Phanagoria

Panticapaeum

Trapezus

Amisus

ASSYRIA

Danube

MOESIA

Serdica

Byzantium

Ancyra

Melitene

Tigris

to Sura

MESOPOTAMIA

Pumbeditha

Prusa

PHRYGIA

Euphrates

MACEDONIA

Tarsus

CILICIA

Dura-Europos

Nehardea

Babylon

Ephesus

CYPRUS

SYRIA

Well-preserved synagogue c.A.D.235

Delos

LYCIA

Damascus

ACHAIA

Tyre

Capernaum

Caesarea

Jamnia

Scythopolis

Hierosolyma (Aelia Capitolina)

School founded by Samuel (180-250)

Jews massacred by Greeks in 66

School for Rabbis after 70

Aelana

Pelusium

Wars against the Romans in A.D. 66-70 and 130-5

Cyrene

Berenice

CYRENAICA

Alexandria

E G Y P T

Nile

Jewish revolt in 116

Jewish revolts in 116

Riots in 66 and community almost wiped out after revolt in 116

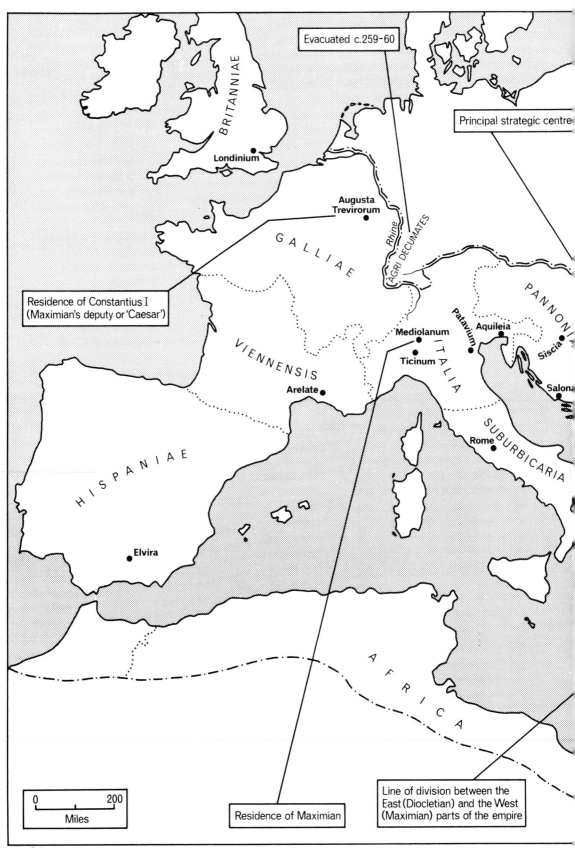

Evacuated c.259-60

Principal strategic centre

Residence of Constantius I
(Maximian's deputy or 'Caesar')

BRITANNIAE

Londinium

Augusta
Trevirorum

GALLIAE

Rhine

AGRI DECUMATES

PANNONI

Patavium

Aquileia

Siscia

Mediolanum

ITALIA

Ticinum

Salona

VIENNENSIS

Arelate

SUBURBICARIA

Rome

HISPANIAE

Elvira

AFRICA

0   200
Miles

Residence of Maximian

Line of division between the
East (Diocletian) and the West
(Maximian) parts of the empire

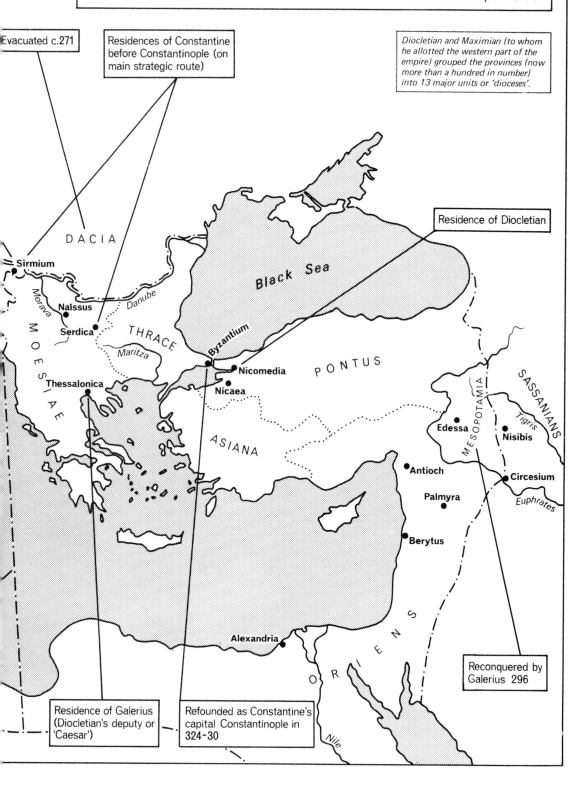

THE ROMAN EMPIRE UNDER
DIOCLETIAN AND MAXIMIAN A.D. 284/6-305

Evacuated c.271

Residences of Constantine
before Constantinople (on
main strategic route)

*Diocletian and Maximian (to whom
he allotted the western part of the
empire) grouped the provinces (now
more than a hundred in number)
into 13 major units or 'dioceses'.*

Residence of Diocletian

DACIA

Sirmium

Morava

Nalssus

Danube

Serdica

THRACE

Maritza

Byzantium

MOESIAE

Thessalonica

Nicomedia

Nicaea

Black Sea

PONTUS

ASIANA

MESOPOTAMIA

SASSANIANS

Tigris

Edessa

Nisibis

Antioch

Circesium

Palmyra

Euphrates

Berytus

ORIENS

Alexandria

Nile

Residence of Galerius
(Diocletian's deputy or
'Caesar')

Refounded as Constantine's
capital Constantinople in
324-30

Reconquered by
Galerius 296

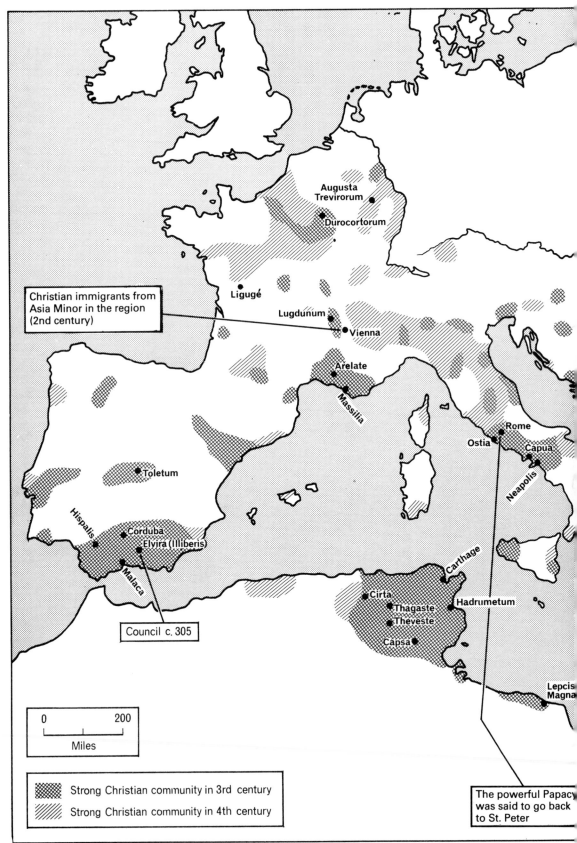

Christian immigrants from
Asia Minor in the region
(2nd century)

Council c. 305

The powerful Papacy
was said to go back
to St. Peter

Augusta
Trevirorum

Durocortorum

Ligugé

Lugdunum

Vienna

Arelate

Massilia

Rome

Ostia

Capua

Neapolis

Toletum

Hispalis

Corduba
Elvira (Illiberis)

Malaca

Carthage

Cirta

Thagaste

Theveste

Hadrumetum

Capsa

Lepcis
Magna

0   200
|————|————|
      Miles

Strong Christian community in 3rd century

Strong Christian community in 4th century

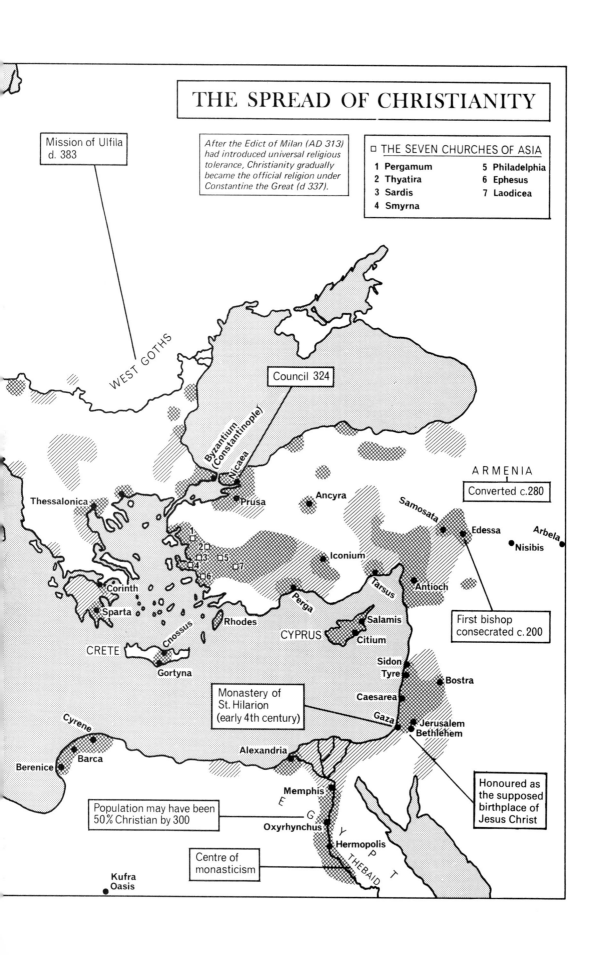

THE SPREAD OF CHRISTIANITY

Mission of Ulfila
d. 383

*After the Edict of Milan (AD 313)
had introduced universal religious
tolerance, Christianity gradually
became the official religion under
Constantine the Great (d 337).*

□ THE SEVEN CHURCHES OF ASIA

1 Pergamum   5 Philadelphia
2 Thyatira   6 Ephesus
3 Sardis   7 Laodicea
4 Smyrna

WEST GOTHS

Council 324

Byzantium
(Constantinople)
Nicaea

ARMENIA
Converted c. 280

Thessalonica

Prusa

Ancyra

Samosata

Edessa

Arbela

Nisibis

1
2
3 □5
4 □6 □7

Iconium

Corinth

Sparta

Rhodes

Perga

Tarsus

Antioch

Salamis

CYPRUS

Citium

First bishop
consecrated c. 200

Cnossus

CRETE

Gortyna

Sidon

Tyre

Bostra

Caesarea

Monastery of
St. Hilarion
(early 4th century)

Gaza

Jerusalem
Bethlehem

Cyrene

Barca

Berenice

Alexandria

Honoured as
the supposed
birthplace of
Jesus Christ

Memphis

E
G

Population may have been
50% Christian by 300

Oxyrhynchus

Y

Hermopolis

P

Centre of
monasticism

THEBAID

T

Kufra
Oasis

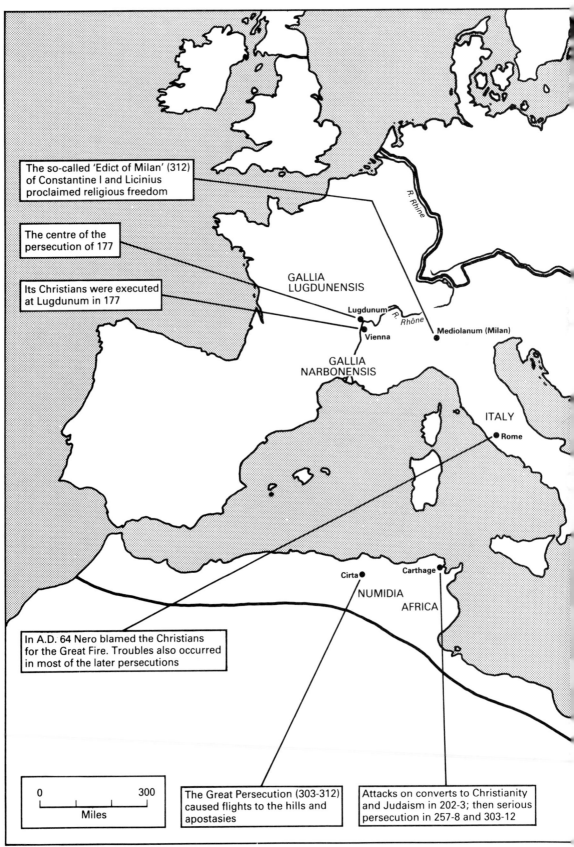

The so-called 'Edict of Milan' (312) of Constantine I and Licinius proclaimed religious freedom

The centre of the persecution of 177

Its Christians were executed at Lugdunum in 177

GALLIA LUGDUNENSIS

Lugdunum

Vienna

Mediolanum (Milan)

GALLIA NARBONENSIS

ITALY

Rome

R. Rhine

R. Rhône

Cirta

Carthage

NUMIDIA

AFRICA

In A.D. 64 Nero blamed the Christians for the Great Fire. Troubles also occurred in most of the later persecutions

0   300
Miles

The Great Persecution (303-312) caused flights to the hills and apostasies

Attacks on converts to Christianity and Judaism in 202-3; then serious persecution in 257-8 and 303-12

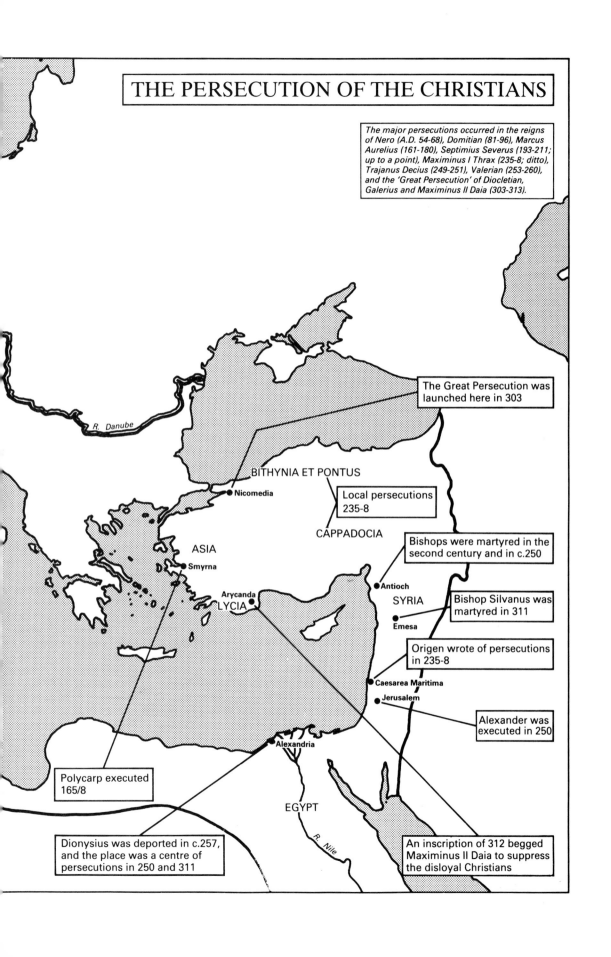

THE PERSECUTION OF THE CHRISTIANS

The major persecutions occurred in the reigns of Nero (A.D. 54-68), Domitian (81-96), Marcus Aurelius (161-180), Septimius Severus (193-211; up to a point), Maximinus I Thrax (235-8; ditto), Trajanus Decius (249-251), Valerian (253-260), and the 'Great Persecution' of Diocletian, Galerius and Maximinus II Daia (303-313).

R. Danube

The Great Persecution was launched here in 303

BITHYNIA ET PONTUS

● Nicomedia

Local persecutions 235-8

CAPPADOCIA

Bishops were martyred in the second century and in c.250

ASIA

● Smyrna

Arycanda ●
LYCIA ●

● Antioch

SYRIA

Bishop Silvanus was martyred in 311

● Emesa

Origen wrote of persecutions in 235-8

● Caesarea Maritima
● Jerusalem

Alexander was executed in 250

● Alexandria

Polycarp executed 165/8

EGYPT

R. Nile

Dionysius was deported in c.257, and the place was a centre of persecutions in 250 and 311

An inscription of 312 begged Maximinus II Daia to suppress the disloyal Christians

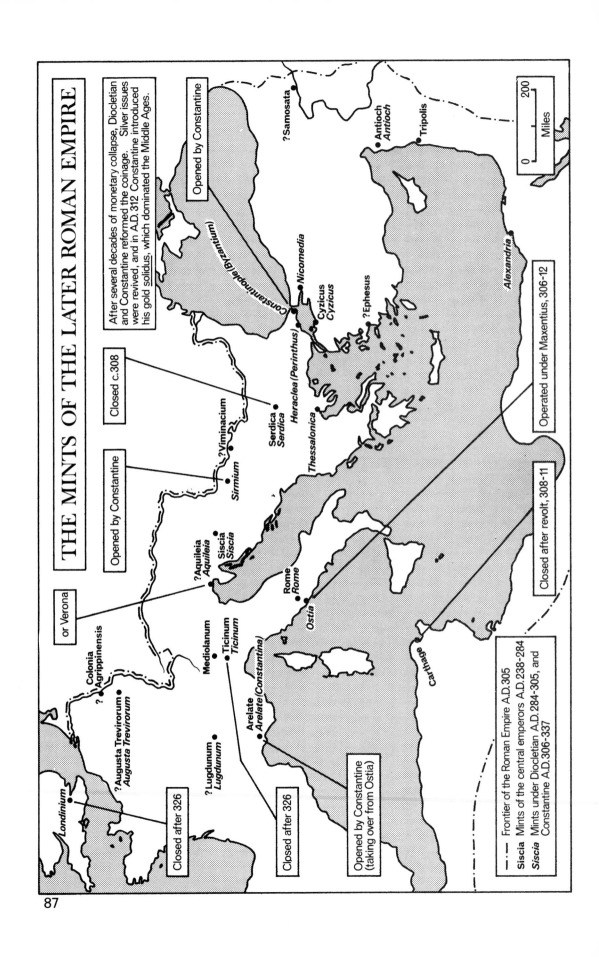

THE MINTS OF THE LATER ROMAN EMPIRE

After several decades of monetary collapse, Diocletian and Constantine reformed the coinage. Silver issues were revived, and in A.D. 312 Constantine introduced his gold solidus, which dominated the Middle Ages.

Opened by Constantine

Closed c.308

Opened by Constantine

or Verona

Colonia
Agrippinensis

?Augusta Treviorum
Augusta Treviorum

?Londinium

?Lugdunum
Lugdunum

Closed after 326

Closed after 326

Mediolanum

Ticinum
Ticinum

Arelate
Arelate (Constantina)

Opened by Constantine
(taking over from Ostia)

?Aquileia
Aquileia

Siscia
Siscia

Rome
Rome

Ostia

Carthage

?Viminacium

Sirmium

Serdica
Serdica

Heraclea (Perinthus)

Thessalonica

Constantinople (Byzantium)

Nicomedia

Cyzicus
Cyzicus

?Ephesus

?Samosata

Antioch
Antioch

Tripolis

Alexandria

Operated under Maxentius, 306-12

Closed after revolt, 308-11

-·-· Frontier of the Roman Empire A.D.305

Siscia Mints of the central emperors A.D.238-284

Siscia Mints under Diocletian A.D. 284-305, and Constantine A.D.306-337

0   200
Miles

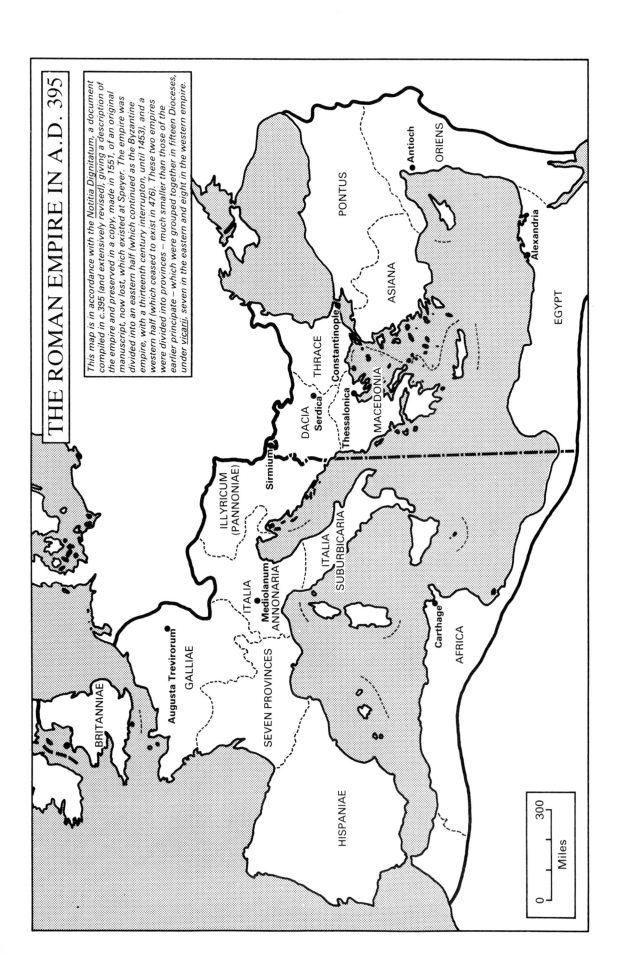

THE ROMAN EMPIRE IN A.D. 395

This map is in accordance with the Notitia Dignitatum, a document compiled in c.395 (and extensively revised), giving a description of the empire and preserved in a copy, made in 1551, of an original manuscript, now lost, which existed at Speyer. The empire was divided into an eastern half (which continued as the Byzantine empire, with a thirteenth century interruption, until 1453), and a western half (which ceased to exist in 476). These two empires were divided into provinces – much smaller than those of the earlier principate – which were grouped together in fifteen Dioceses, under vicarii, seven in the eastern and eight in the western empire.

BRITANNIAE

GALLIAE

Augusta Trevirorum

SEVEN PROVINCES

ITALIA

Mediolanum
ANNONARIA

HISPANIAE

ITALIA
SUBURBICARIA

AFRICA

Carthage

ILLYRICUM
(PANNONIAE)

Sirmium

DACIA

Serdica

THRACE

Constantinople

Thessalonica

MACEDONIA

PONTUS

ASIANA

ORIENS

Antioch

Alexandria

EGYPT

0   300

Miles

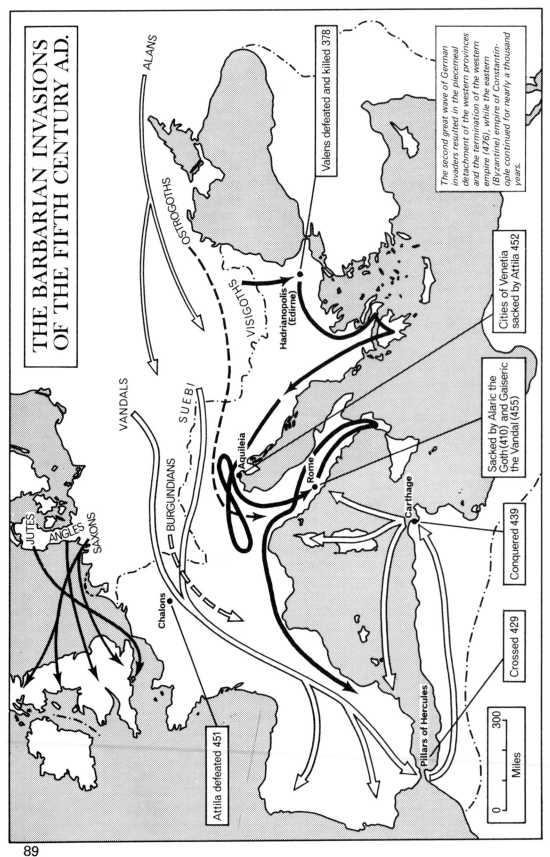

THE BARBARIAN INVASIONS OF THE FIFTH CENTURY A.D.

ALANS

OSTROGOTHS

VISIGOTHS

Valens defeated and killed 378

Hadrianopolis (Edirne)

VANDALS

SUEBI

BURGUNDIANS

Aquileia

Rome

Cities of Venetia sacked by Attila 452

Sacked by Alaric the Goth (410) and Gaiseric the Vandal (455)

Carthage

Conquered 439

JUTES

ANGLES

SAXONS

Chalons

Attila defeated 451

Crossed 429

Pillars of Hercules

The second great wave of German invaders resulted in the piecemeal detachment of the western provinces and the termination of the western empire (476), while the eastern (Byzantine) empire of Constantinople continued for nearly a thousand years.

0   300

Miles

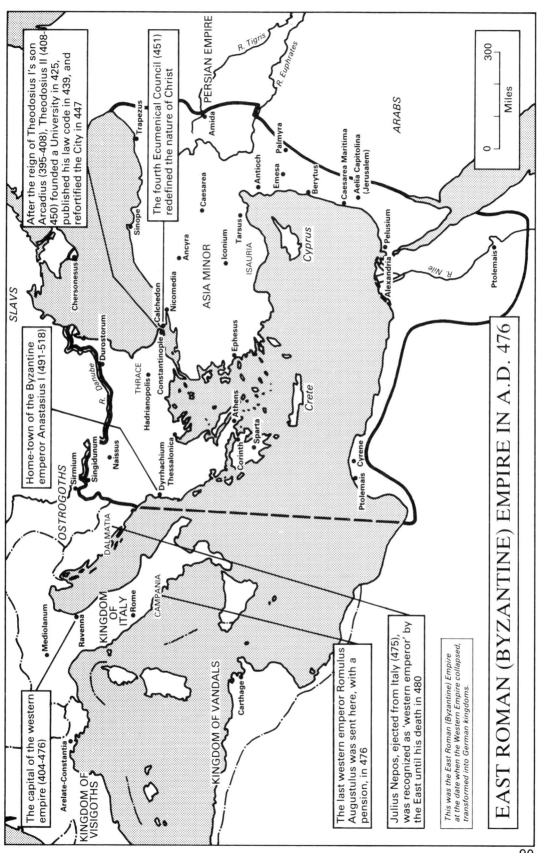

SLAVS

PERSIAN EMPIRE

R. Tigris

R. Euphrates

ARABS

After the reign of Theodosius I's son Arcadius (395-408), Theodosius II (408-450) founded a University in 425, published his law code in 439, and refortified the City in 447

The fourth Ecumenical Council (451) redefined the nature of Christ

Home-town of the Byzantine emperor Anastasius I (491-518)

The capital of the western empire (404-476)

The last western emperor Romulus Augustulus was sent here, with a pension, in 476

Julius Nepos, ejected from Italy (475), was recognized as 'western emperor' by the East until his death in 480

This was the East Roman (Byzantine) Empire at the date when the Western Empire collapsed, transformed into German kingdoms.

0   300
Miles

Trapezus
Amida
Palmyra
Caesarea
Antioch
Emesa
Berytus
Caesarea Maritima
Aelia Capitolina (Jerusalem)
Sinope
Ancyra
Iconium
Tarsus
ISAURIA
Cyprus
Pelusium
R. Nile
Ptolemais
Alexandria

ASIA MINOR

Calchedon
Nicomedia
Chersonesus
Durostorum
R. Danube
THRACE
Hadrianopolis
Constantinople
Ephesus
Athens
Corinth
Sparta
Crete

Sirmium
Singidunum
Naissus
Dyrrhachium
Thessalonica
Ptolemais
Cyrene

OSTROGOTHS

DALMATIA

Mediolanum
Ravenna
KINGDOM OF ITALY
Rome
CAMPANIA

Arelate-Constantia
KINGDOM OF VISIGOTHS

KINGDOM OF VANDALS
Carthage

EAST ROMAN (BYZANTINE) EMPIRE IN A.D. 476

90

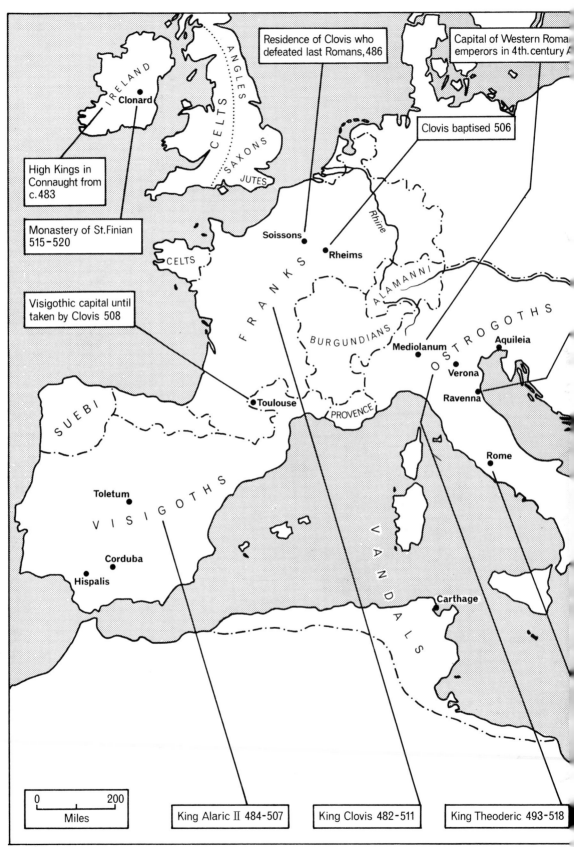

Residence of Clovis who defeated last Romans, 486

Capital of Western Roma[n] emperors in 4th. century A[D]

Clovis baptised 506

High Kings in Connaught from c.483

Monastery of St.Finian 515-520

Visigothic capital until taken by Clovis 508

IRELAND

Clonard

ANGLES

CELTS

SAXONS

JUTES

CELTS

Soissons

Rheims

Rhine

FRANKS

ALAMANNI

BURGUNDIANS

OSTROGOTHS

Mediolanum

Aquileia

Verona

Ravenna

Toulouse

PROVENCE

SUEBI

VISIGOTHS

Toletum

Corduba

Hispalis

VANDALS

Rome

Carthage

0   200
Miles

King Alaric II 484-507

King Clovis 482-511

King Theoderic 493-518

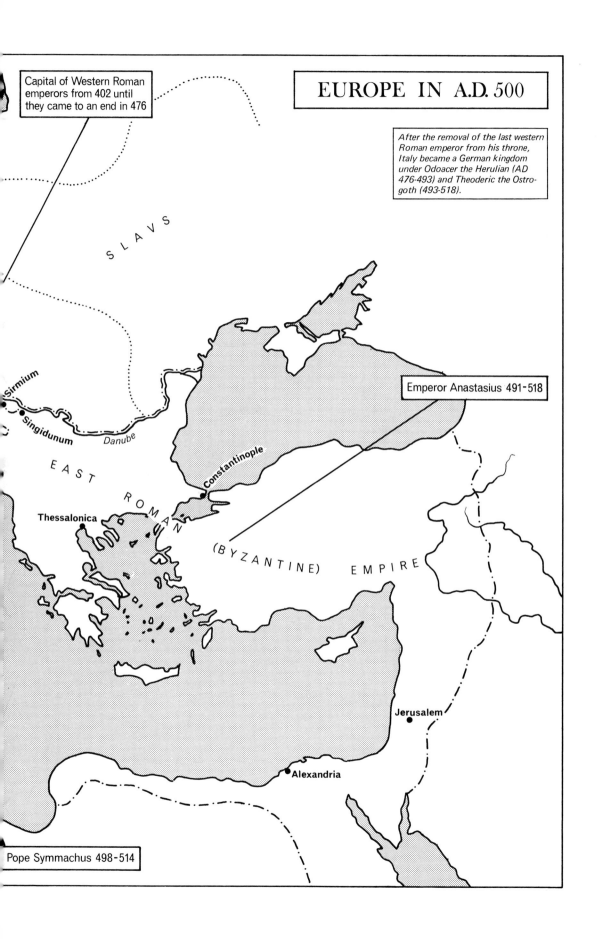

EUROPE IN A.D. 500

Capital of Western Roman emperors from 402 until they came to an end in 476

After the removal of the last western Roman emperor from his throne, Italy became a German kingdom under Odoacer the Herulian (AD 476-493) and Theoderic the Ostrogoth (493-518).

SLAVS

Sirmium

Singidunum

Danube

EAST

ROMAN

Constantinople

Thessalonica

(BYZANTINE)   EMPIRE

Emperor Anastasius 491-518

Jerusalem

Alexandria

Pope Symmachus 498-514

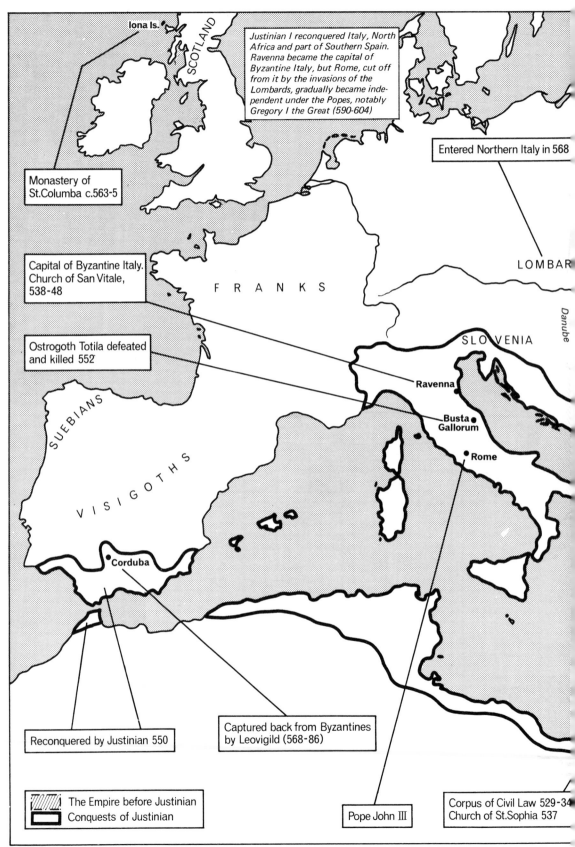

Iona Is.

SCOTLAND

Justinian I reconquered Italy, North
Africa and part of Southern Spain.
Ravenna became the capital of
Byzantine Italy, but Rome, cut off
from it by the invasions of the
Lombards, gradually became inde-
pendent under the Popes, notably
Gregory I the Great (590-604)

Entered Northern Italy in 568

Monastery of
St.Columba c.563-5

LOMBAR

FRANKS

Danube

Capital of Byzantine Italy.
Church of San Vitale,
538-48

SLOVENIA

Ostrogoth Totila defeated
and killed 552

Ravenna

Busta
Gallorum

SUEBIANS

Rome

VISIGOTHS

Corduba

Reconquered by Justinian 550

Captured back from Byzantines
by Leovigild (568-86)

The Empire before Justinian
Conquests of Justinian

Pope John III

Corpus of Civil Law 529-34
Church of St.Sophia 537

92

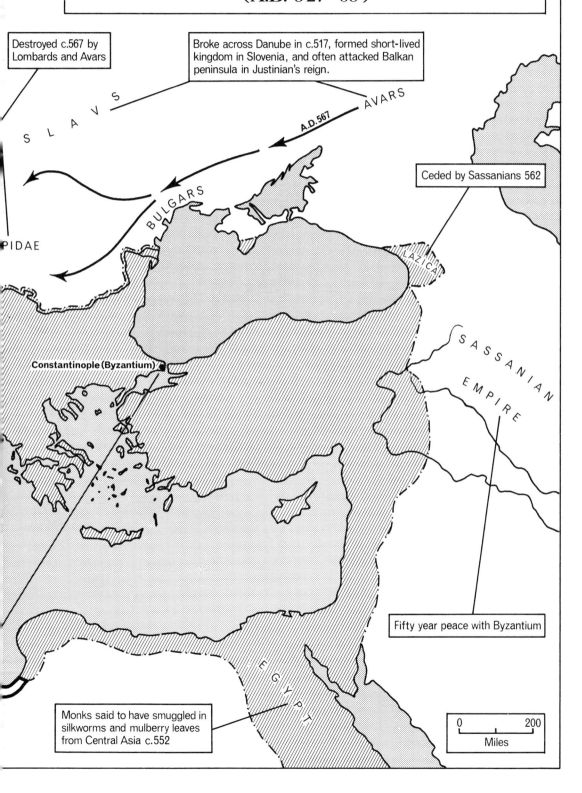

THE BYZANTINE EMPIRE OF JUSTINIAN I
(A.D. 527-65)

Destroyed c.567 by Lombards and Avars

Broke across Danube in c.517, formed short-lived kingdom in Slovenia, and often attacked Balkan peninsula in Justinian's reign.

SLAVS

AVARS

A.D. 567

Ceded by Sassanians 562

BULGARS

PIDAE

LAZICA

Constantinople (Byzantium)

SASSANIAN EMPIRE

Fifty year peace with Byzantium

EGYPT

Monks said to have smuggled in silkworms and mulberry leaves from Central Asia c.552

0   200
Miles

Index of Place Names[1]

Modern names are given in brackets

[1] I have sometimes sacrificed consistency of spelling to convenience and tradition.